Gooseberry Patch

An imprint of Globe Pequot
64 South Main Street
Essex, CT 06426

www.gooseberrypatch.com

1•800•854•6673

Copyright 2023, Gooseberry Patch 978-1-62093-530-9
Photo Edition is a major revision of **Farmhouse Kitchen**.

Do you have a tried & true recipe...

tip, craft or memory that you'd like to see featured in
a **Gooseberry Patch** cookbook? Visit our website at
www.gooseberrypatch.com and follow the
easy steps to submit your favorite family recipe.

Or send them to us at:

Gooseberry Patch
PO Box 812
Columbus, OH 43216-0812

Don't forget to include the number of servings your recipe
makes, plus your name, address, phone number and
email address. If we select your recipe, your name will
appear right along with it...and you'll receive
a **FREE** copy of the book!

Contents

Dedication

To everyone who loves sweet country
air and the taste of a fresh-baked
slice of cherry pie.

Appreciation

A big country thanks to each of our
friends for sharing your best
home-cooked recipes.

Farm-Fresh
Breakfasts

Grandma Hopkins' French Toast
Farrah Richards
Kinsman, OH

My mom got this recipe from her mother-in-law. I grew up on a farm and we would often have this on Saturday mornings after morning chores. Just knowing that we were going to have French toast afterwards made us do our chores a little faster. Now I fix it for my husband and little boy...they love it too!

2 eggs, beaten
1 c. milk
1 c. all-purpose flour
2 t. sugar
1/2 t. baking powder
1/4 t. salt

1/2 t. nutmeg
1/2 t. cinnamon
8 to 10 slices Texas toast
Optional: bacon drippings
Garnish: maple syrup

Whisk together eggs and milk in a small bowl; set aside. In a large shallow bowl, mix flour, sugar, baking powder, salt and spices. Add egg mixture to flour mixture to make a thin batter. Dip bread slices into batter. Heat drippings, if using, or non-stick vegetable spray on a griddle over medium heat. Fry bread slices on both sides until golden. Serve with maple syrup. Makes 8 to 10 servings.

Start a collection of retro jelly-jar juice glasses...
their fun designs and bright colors will make
everyone smile at breakfast time.

Farm-Fresh *Breakfasts*

Cinnamon Sticky Buns

Ruby Dorosh
Shippensburg, PA

These yummy buns are a snap to make with frozen bread dough.

1/2 c. brown sugar, packed
1/2 c. molasses
1/2 c. butter, melted and divided

1/2 c. cinnamon-sugar
2 loaves frozen bread dough,
   thawed

Combine brown sugar, molasses and 1/4 cup butter in an ungreased 13"x9" baking pan. Place in a 325-degree oven until melted. Remove from oven; stir to mix and set aside. Place remaining butter in a small dish; place cinnamon-sugar in another small dish. Pinch off bite-size pieces of dough; dip each piece into melted butter, then roll in cinnamon-sugar. Place dough pieces in pan on top of brown sugar mixture. Cover pan; let stand until dough rises to top of pan, about one hour. Bake at 325 degrees for 35 minutes. Immediately invert pan onto a tray; let sticky glaze drizzle over buns. Makes 8 to 10 servings.

Vintage rotary mixers can be found at flea markets and tag sales. They're oh-so handy for mixing up pancake batter and scrambling eggs quickly and easily.

Betty's Hot Cheese Toast

Connie Chambers
Colorado City, TX

*A wonderful friend of mine would always share this scrumptious dish
when she hosted our ladies' Bible studies. It is so good...we all loved
walking into her kitchen and smelling the hot cheese toast in the oven!*

1 c. mayonnaise
2 t. Worcestershire sauce
1/2 t. ranch salad dressing mix
1/4 t. paprika
2 green onions, chopped

2-1/2 oz. pkg. chopped almonds
8-oz. pkg. shredded Cheddar
  cheese
2 T. bacon bits
15 bread slices, halved

Combine all ingredients except bread slices; mix well. Spread on
half-slices of bread; arrange slices on a lightly greased baking sheet.
Bake for 10 minutes at 400 degrees, until golden. Serve hot. Makes
12 to 15 servings.

A wire basket full of brown eggs makes a terrific farm-style
breakfast centerpiece. For a seasonal touch, fill the basket
with mini white eggplants or egg-shaped gourds.

Farm-Fresh *Breakfasts*

Hearty Sausage & Egg Bake

Laura Phares
Greenfield, IN

This easy-to-fix dish is always a big hit when I serve it at our church's sunrise breakfast...everyone just loves it!

6-oz. pkg. croutons
2 lbs. ground pork sausage,
   browned and drained
6 eggs, beaten
2-1/2 c. milk

1 t. dry mustard
10-3/4 oz. can cream of
   mushroom soup
8-oz. pkg. shredded Cheddar
   cheese

The night before, sprinkle croutons into a greased 13"x9" baking pan; top with sausage. Beat eggs, milk and mustard together; pour over sausage. Cover and refrigerate overnight. In the morning, spread soup over casserole; sprinkle with cheese. Bake, uncovered, at 300 degrees for one hour, or until center is done. Makes 16 servings.

A buttery slice of cinnamon toast warms you right up on a chilly morning. Spread softened butter generously on one side of toasted white bread and sprinkle with cinnamon-sugar. Broil for one to 2 minutes until hot and bubbly. Serve with mugs of hot cocoa...yummy!

Chocolate Chip Scones

Terry Parke
Indianapolis, IN

For a tasty variation, use white chocolate chips instead of milk chocolate...even add some dried cherries or blueberries.

1 c. sour cream or buttermilk
1 t. baking soda
4 c. all-purpose flour
1 c. sugar
2 t. baking powder
1/4 t. cream of tartar

1 t. salt
1 c. butter
1 c. milk chocolate chips
1 egg, beaten
1 T. vanilla extract
Garnish: sugar

Stir together sour cream or buttermilk and baking soda in a small bowl; set aside. In a large bowl, combine flour, sugar, baking powder, cream of tartar and salt. Cut in butter with a pastry blender; mix in chocolate chips. Add egg and vanilla to sour cream mixture; stir into dry ingredients just until moistened. Turn dough out onto a lightly floured surface; roll or pat out into a round about 3/4-inch thick. Cut into wedges or cut out circles with a large round cookie cutter. Place on 2 lightly greased baking sheets; sprinkle with sugar. Bake at 350 degrees for 12 to 15 minutes, or until golden. Makes about one dozen.

Share your homemade goodies with a friend. Wrap scones in a tea towel and tuck them into a basket along with a jar of jam. A sweet gift that says, "I'm thinking of you!"

Farm-Fresh *Breakfasts*

Apple-Cinnamon Spread

Francie Stutzman
Dalton, OH

Scrumptious on raisin bread or toasted bagels.

2 8-oz. pkgs. cream cheese,
    softened
1 apple, cored, peeled and diced
1/2 c. raisins

1/4 c. orange marmalade
1/2 t. cinnamon
1/8 t. nutmeg

Combine all ingredients and stir until well blended. Spoon into a covered container; keep refrigerated. Makes about 3 cups.

I'll tell you how the sun rose,
A ribbon at a time.
– Emily Dickinson

Creamy Ambrosia Salad

Amber Carlson
Irvine, CA

On busy mornings, I love having a big bowl of this sweet, healthy fruit salad ready for my family's breakfast. It only requires a handful of ingredients and takes just minutes to put together.

1/2 c. mayonnaise
1 c. plain or vanilla yogurt
30-oz. can fruit cocktail, drained
20-oz. can pineapple chunks,
   drained

5-oz. pkg. sweetened flaked
   coconut
1/2 c. raisins
1/2 c. chopped walnuts

In a large bowl, fold mayonnaise into yogurt. Stir in remaining ingredients. Cover and refrigerate for 2 hours, or until thoroughly chilled. Makes 8 to 10 servings.

Tuck fresh blossoms into vintage soda bottles to line up
on a windowsill. Tint the water in the bottles with
a few drops of food coloring, just for fun.

Farm-Fresh *Breakfasts*

Peach Cobbler Muffins

Bonnie Allard
Santa Rosa, CA

My most requested muffins...I hope you all like them as much as my family & friends do! Everyone loves them so much, they disappear right away whenever I make them to share.

3 c. all-purpose flour
1 c. sugar
1-1/2 T. baking soda
1/2 t. salt

3/4 c. butter, diced
1-3/4 c. milk
16-oz. can peaches, drained and chopped

Mix flour, sugar, baking soda and salt in a large bowl. Cut in butter with a pastry knife or a fork. Add milk and peaches; stir just until moistened. Spoon batter into greased or paper-lined muffin cups, filling 2/3 full. Spoon topping onto muffins. Bake at 400 degrees for about 20 minutes, or until golden. Turn out and cool slightly on a wire rack; serve warm or cold. Makes 1-1/2 dozen.

Topping:

2 T. butter, diced
2 T. sugar

1/2 t. cinnamon

Mix together in a small bowl until crumbly.

Most muffin batters can be stirred up the night before, and can even be scooped into muffin cups. Simply cover and refrigerate...in the morning, pop them in the oven. Your family will love waking up to the sweet smell of muffins baking!

Blueberry-Sausage Breakfast Cake *Sarah Hoechst*
Bismarck, ND

An all-in-one breakfast that's extra special.

2 c. all-purpose flour
1 t. baking powder
1/2 t. baking soda
1/2 c. butter
3/4 c. sugar
1/4 c. brown sugar, packed

8-oz. container sour cream
2 eggs
1 lb. ground pork sausage,
   browned and drained
1 c. blueberries
1/2 c. chopped pecans

In a medium bowl, mix flour, baking powder and baking soda; set aside. In a large bowl, beat butter until fluffy with an electric mixer on medium speed. Add sugars and sour cream; beat until combined. Add eggs, one at a time, beating just until combined. Add butter mixture to flour mixture. Fold in sausage and berries. Pour batter into an ungreased 13"x9" baking pan. Spread evenly in pan; sprinkle pecans on top. Bake at 350 degrees for 35 to 40 minutes, until a toothpick comes out clean. Cool on a wire rack; cut into squares. Serve with warm Blueberry Sauce. Makes 15 servings.

Blueberry Sauce:

1/2 c. sugar
2 T. cornstarch
1/2 c. water

2 c. blueberries
1/2 c. lemon juice

Combine sugar and cornstarch in a medium saucepan; add water and berries. Cook and stir over medium heat until thickened and bubbly. Cook and stir 2 minutes more. Stir in lemon juice; cool slightly before pouring over cake.

Add a dash of whimsy to the breakfast table...serve up cream or pancake syrup in a vintage cow-shaped creamer.

Farm-Fresh *Breakfasts*

Harriet's Potato Pancakes

Harriet Hughes
Wurtsboro, NY

My husband loved to eat one pancake between two buttered pieces of bread with a cup of coffee...anytime! These are so good. I passed this recipe along to our niece who owns a cafe, and they are one of her breakfast hits.

1 c. all-purpose flour
2 t. baking powder
Optional: 1 t. salt
2 eggs, beaten
1 c. milk

2 T. onion, grated
1/4 c. butter, melted
3 c. potatoes, peeled and finely
   grated
additional butter for frying

In a small bowl, mix together flour, baking powder and salt, if using; set aside. Combine remaining ingredients, except butter for frying, together in a medium bowl. Stir flour mixture into potato mixture until well blended. Drop by tablespoonfuls onto a buttered frying pan or griddle. Cook on both sides until golden. Serves 6.

A hearty breakfast that's welcome on the chilliest morning! Cook up frozen diced potatoes and onions in a cast-iron skillet, then use the back of a spoon to make 6 wells. Break an egg into each and bake at 350 degrees for 12 to 14 minutes, until eggs are set. Add salt & pepper to taste and serve piping hot, right from the skillet.

Crispy Cornbread Waffles

Cathy Clemons
Narrows, VA

I served these yummy waffles when my son and his family came in for the weekend. My grandbabies just loved these with apple butter... I didn't think they would ever get full!

10 slices bacon
1/3 c. oil
2 c. cornmeal
1 c. all-purpose flour
1 t. baking powder
1/2 t. baking soda
1/2 t. salt

2 t. sugar
1-1/2 c. milk
2 T. white vinegar
2 eggs
Garnish: butter, apple butter,
    maple syrup

Fry bacon in a large skillet over medium heat; remove bacon and crumble. Stir oil into drippings; set aside to cool. In a medium bowl, combine cornmeal, flour, baking powder, baking soda, salt and sugar; set aside. Combine milk and vinegar; let stand for 10 minutes. Beat eggs in a large bowl; add drippings and milk mixture. Add cornmeal mixture and crumbled bacon; mix well. Pour by 1/4 or 1/2 cupfuls onto a preheated waffle iron. Bake until golden, according to manufacturer's directions. Serve with butter and apple butter or maple syrup. Makes about 5 servings.

Waffles with whipped cream and fruit...is there a more delicious way to start a day? We don't think so! Garden-fresh strawberries and blueberries are irresistible...thawed frozen berries are yummy too and available year 'round.

Farm-Fresh *Breakfasts*

Mom's Red Flannel Hash

Phyllis Peters
Three Rivers, MI

This is an old family recipe that has stayed a favorite through the generations. It's a good way to use up leftover cooked potatoes. A real down-home breakfast dish...give it a try!

12-oz. can corned beef, coarsely chopped
2 c. beets, peeled, cooked and chopped

2 c. potatoes, peeled, cooked and chopped
1/2 c. butter, melted

Toss all ingredients together. Pour into a greased 2-quart casserole dish. Bake, uncovered, at 350 degrees for 40 minutes. Makes 4 to 6 servings.

Hard-boiled eggs the easy way! Cover eggs with an inch of water in a saucepan; place over medium-high heat. As soon as the water boils, cover the pan and remove from heat. Let stand for 18 to 20 minutes...cover with ice water, peel and they're done!

Angel Biscuits

Molly Wilson
Rapid City, SD

My mother would make this up every Sunday afternoon so we could have fresh-baked bread all week. The dough will keep for several weeks in the refrigerator.

2 envs. active dry yeast
1 c. warm water
2 c. buttermilk
3/4 c. oil
1/4 c. sugar

6 c. all-purpose flour
4 t. baking powder
1/4 t. baking soda
1-1/2 t. salt

In a very large bowl, dissolve yeast in very warm water, 110 to 115 degrees; let stand for several minutes. Stir in buttermilk, oil and sugar. In a large bowl, combine remaining ingredients; stir into buttermilk mixture. Cover bowl and place in refrigerator overnight. Remove dough as needed. Roll out on a floured board to 1/2-inch thickness. Cut out biscuits with a round biscuit cutter or a glass tumbler; place on an ungreased baking sheet. Bake at 400 degrees for 12 to 15 minutes, until golden. Makes 4 dozen.

Shh...here's the secret to flaky homemade biscuits!
Don't overmix or overwork the dough...just stir
to mix and roll or pat out gently.

Farm-Fresh *Breakfasts*

Mama's Tomato Gravy

Melissa Dommert
Baytown, TX

My mama, Patsy Marie Paul, made countless batches of biscuits and tomato gravy in her lifetime. I'm sure she learned to make this from her mother, Carmen Inez Shirley. It's a genuine taste of Louisiana Cajun country, where folks are already drinking coffee and eating breakfast by the time the rooster crows.

1/4 c. bacon drippings
3 T. all-purpose flour
2 c. water

5 T. tomato paste
salt and pepper to taste
6 to 8 buttermilk biscuits, split

Heat drippings in a skillet over medium-high heat. Stir in flour and cook, stirring constantly, until lightly golden. Slowly pour water into flour mixture while whisking; whisk in tomato paste. Cook mixture until it begins to thicken. Reduce heat to low and simmer until thick, about 5 minutes. Add salt and pepper to taste. Spoon over biscuits. Makes 6 to 8 servings.

Salt & pepper is a must with scrambled eggs, crispy hashbrowns and other tasty breakfast foods. Look for a pair of rooster-shaped shakers for a sweet rise & shine greeting at the breakfast table.

Grandma's Doughnut Holes

Lillian Child
Omaha, NE

My Grandma Karaus brought these fresh, hot doughnut holes to every family gathering. We kids always looked forward to seeing that large brown grocery sack full of these sugary treats!

1-1/2 c. all-purpose flour
1/3 c. sugar
2 t. baking powder
1/2 t. salt
1/2 t. nutmeg
1/2 c. milk

2 T. oil
1 t. vanilla extract
1 egg, beaten
oil for deep frying
Garnish: 1/2 c. sugar,
   1 T. cinnamon

Combine flour, sugar, baking powder, salt and nutmeg in a large bowl; set aside. In a small bowl, whisk together milk, oil, vanilla and egg. Add milk mixture to dry ingredients. Stir with a fork just until dry ingredients are moistened; do not overmix. Heat 3 to 4 inches oil to 375 degrees in a large saucepan. Drop batter by teaspoonfuls into hot oil, 5 to 6 at a time. Fry one to 2 minutes on each side, until deep golden. Drain on paper towels. Mix sugar and cinnamon; place in a brown paper bag. Drop warm doughnut holes into bag; shake until coated. Makes 3 dozen.

Float a blossom inside a 1950's-era egg cup to set
at each breakfast place...so cheerful!

French Breakfast Puffs

Andrea Cullinan
Delaware, OH

My family has always enjoyed these melt-in-your-mouth muffins.
If making mini muffins, reduce the temperature to 325 degrees
and bake for 10 to 12 minutes.

1/3 c. shortening	1/2 t. salt
1 c. sugar, divided	1/2 t. nutmeg
1 egg, beaten	1/2 c. milk
1-1/2 c. all-purpose flour	1 t. cinnamon
1-1/2 t. baking powder	6 T. butter, melted

Blend together shortening, 1/2 cup sugar and egg in a large bowl; set aside. In another large bowl, combine flour, baking powder, salt and nutmeg. Add to shortening mixture alternately with milk; stir until moistened. Fill greased muffin cups 2/3 full. Bake at 350 degrees for 20 to 25 minutes, until golden. Combine cinnamon and remaining sugar. Roll hot muffins in melted butter and then in cinnamon-sugar mixture. Makes one dozen.

Vintage glass measuring cups are a real find at tag sales! Look for them in rosy pink and leafy green tints as well as milk glass and jadeite. Use one-cup measures to serve up cream & sugar...tuck bouquets of freshly cut flowers into oversized 4-cup measures.

Mom's Everything Waffles

Tamara Ahrens
Sparta, MI

These waffles have been a Saturday morning tradition in our family since our children were very little. If a week goes by without our waffles, we try to slip them in for a weeknight meal. They have developed over time with the addition of many tasty ingredients...even chocolate chips for birthdays and Christmas!

2 c. biscuit baking mix
1-1/2 c. quick-cooking oats, uncooked
1/4 c. wheat germ
1/2 c. chopped pecans or walnuts
2 eggs, beaten
1/4 c. peanut butter

1/2 c. vanilla yogurt
3-1/2 c. low-fat milk, divided
1 c. blueberries
Optional: 1/4 c. mini chocolate chips
Garnish: maple syrup, fruit topping, whipped cream

Combine baking mix, oats, wheat germ and nuts in a large bowl; set aside. In a separate bowl, whisk together eggs, peanut butter, yogurt and 3 cups milk. Add to dry ingredients and stir. Add additional milk if needed to get the consistency of applesauce. Fold in berries and chocolate chips, if using. Pour by 1/2 cupfuls onto a preheated waffle iron that has been sprayed with non-stick vegetable spray. Bake until crisp, according to manufacturer's directions. Serve with maple syrup or fruit topping and a dollop of whipped cream. Serves 4 to 6.

A jar of honey is a sweet addition to the breakfast table to enjoy on hot biscuits, toast or pancakes...even drizzled in a steamy cup of hot tea. For a sweet gift, pick up flavors like orange blossom and wildflower at a farmers' market...be sure to add a wooden honey dipper too!

Farm-Fresh *Breakfasts*

Ma Carrico's Buttermilk Pancakes

Sheila Cope
Colorado Springs, CO

These pancakes are the best! I got this recipe from Irene Carrico, who has since passed away, while I was working for her at the Arctic Circle Restaurant in Kanab, Utah. "Ma" made these for me every morning... sometimes she would spoil me by adding mashed bananas to the batter and drizzling strawberry syrup over the top.

1 c. all-purpose flour
1 t. baking powder
1/4 t. baking soda
1/2 t. salt

1 c. buttermilk
1 egg, beaten
3 T. sugar
3 T. oil

Combine all ingredients; mix well. Pour by 1/4 cupfuls on a hot griddle sprayed with non-stick vegetable spray over medium heat. Cook pancakes until golden and bubbles appear around edges; flip and cook other side. Makes 12 to 15, 4-inch pancakes.

Homemade pancakes on a weekday morning...what a treat! Pancakes can be stored in plastic freezer bags for up to a month. To serve, place pancakes in a single layer on a baking sheet, cover with aluminum foil and bake at 350 degrees for about 10 minutes. Please pass the syrup!

Marine Corps Breakfast

Marilyn Miller
Fort Washington, PA

From my dad's days in the U.S. Marine Corps...anyone with a hearty appetite will appreciate this old favorite!

1/2 lb. ground beef
1 T. bacon drippings
1/8 t. salt
3 T. all-purpose flour

2 c. milk
salt and pepper to taste
8 slices white bread, toasted

In a large skillet over medium heat, brown and crumble ground beef with drippings and salt. Remove skillet from heat; let cool slightly. Mix in flour until all of the beef is covered. Return skillet to medium heat and stir in milk. Cook and stir until mixture comes to a boil and thickens; boil for at least one minute. Serve over toast. Serves 2 hungry Marines or 8 regular diners.

Red-Eye Gravy & Biscuits

Stacie Avner
Delaware, OH

My grandma lived in Kentucky and whenever we visited her, my dad would pick up a country ham to bring home. This was my favorite breakfast that my dad made for us on chilly mornings.

2 T. butter
6 slices country-style ham
1 T. all-purpose flour
1 c. strong brewed coffee
1-1/2 T. brown sugar, packed

1/2 c. water
salt and pepper to taste
Optional: hot pepper sauce
 to taste
6 biscuits, split and buttered

Melt butter in a skillet over medium-high heat. Cook ham slices until lightly browned; remove from skillet. Add flour to drippings in skillet; cook and stir for one minute. Add coffee, brown sugar and water. Cook and stir for 3 minutes, until thickened; return ham to skillet. Stir in seasonings. Serve ham and gravy over biscuits. Serves 6.

Farm-Fresh *Breakfasts*

Sausage & Cheddar Grits

Sharon Brown
Orange Park, FL

A rich, savory version of a southern favorite...yum!

4 c. water
1 t. salt
1 c. quick-cooking grits,
  uncooked
4 eggs, beaten
1 lb. ground pork sausage,
  browned and drained

1-1/2 c. shredded Cheddar
  cheese, divided
1 c. milk
1/4 c. butter

Bring water and salt to boil in a large saucepan over medium heat. Stir in grits; cook for 4 to 5 minutes. Remove from heat. Stir a small amount of hot grits mixture into eggs; stir egg mixture into saucepan. Add sausage, one cup cheese, milk and butter; blend together well. Pour into a greased 13"x9" baking pan. Sprinkle with remaining cheese. Bake, uncovered, at 350 degrees for one hour, or until cheese is golden. If cheese is getting golden early, cover with aluminum foil. Let cool for about 10 minutes before serving. Serves 6 to 8.

A quick, no-mess way to cook bacon. Arrange bacon slices on a broiler pan and place the pan 3 to 4 inches from the preheated broiler. Broil for one to 2 minutes on each side, depending on how crispy you like your bacon.

Just Peachy French Toast

Vickie
Gooseberry Patch

Top with a dollop of whipped cream...scrumptious!

1 c. brown sugar, packed
1/2 c. butter
2 T. water
29-oz. can sliced peaches,
   drained

12 slices day-old French bread
5 eggs, beaten
1 T. vanilla extract
cinnamon to taste
Garnish: maple syrup

The night before, combine brown sugar, butter and water in a saucepan; bring to a boil. Reduce heat to low; cook for 10 minutes, stirring frequently. Pour into a greased 13"x9" baking pan, tilting to coat bottom of pan. Arrange peaches in pan; top with bread and set aside. Whisk together eggs and vanilla; pour over bread to coat evenly. Sprinkle with cinnamon. Cover and refrigerate overnight. In the morning, let stand at room temperature for 30 minutes. Uncover and bake at 350 degrees for 25 to 30 minutes, until golden. Serve with syrup. Makes 8 servings.

Marlene's Pancake Syrup

Beth Bundy
Long Prairie, MN

This recipe was created by my mother many years ago...
it brings back warm, sticky memories!

2 c. sugar
1 c. brown sugar, packed
1-1/2 c. water

2 T. corn syrup
1 t. maple flavoring

In a medium saucepan over medium heat, stir together all ingredients except maple flavoring. Simmer for 5 minutes; add flavoring. Stir to combine and serve. Refrigerate any leftovers. Makes 3 cups.

For a change, try an old farmhouse tradition...a big slice of apple or cherry pie for breakfast!

Farm-Fresh *Breakfasts*

Trudy's Cherry Coffee Cake

Dawn Menard
Seekonk, MA

This was given to me by my friend Kelley...it's a recipe from her mother Trudy. I like to make it with different fruit fillings like blueberry or apple and various nuts like pecans or almonds. My son requests it often!

1 egg, beaten
1/4 c. milk
1/2 c. sugar
1/8 t. salt
1/2 t. vanilla extract
1-3/4 c. biscuit baking mix, divided

21-oz. can cherry pie filling, partially drained
1/2 c. brown sugar, packed
1/2 t. cinnamon
3 T. butter, diced
1/3 c. chopped walnuts

Combine egg, milk, sugar, salt, vanilla and 1-1/2 cups baking mix. Stir until smooth. Pour mixture into a lightly greased 8"x8" baking pan. Spoon pie filling over mixture in pan. Mix together remaining baking mix, brown sugar, cinnamon, butter and nuts. Sprinkle over pie filling. Bake at 375 degrees for 30 minutes. Cut into squares. Makes 6 to 8 servings.

Looking for a new family message board? Hang an old-fashioned washboard for a whimsical way to keep notes organized. Just use magnets to keep messages and photos secure.

Walnut-Maple Streusel Cake

Sarah Oravecz
Gooseberry Patch

*A delectable sweet treat any time of day! This cake keeps well,
so feel free to bake it the day before and store it,
wrapped in plastic, at room temperature.*

2 c. all-purpose flour
1 t. baking powder
1 t. baking soda
1/2 t. salt
3/4 c. sugar

1/2 c. butter, room temperature
2 eggs, beaten
1 t. vanilla extract
8-oz. container sour cream

Whisk together flour, baking powder, baking soda and salt in a
medium bowl; set aside. In a large bowl, with an electric mixer on
medium-high speed, beat sugar and butter until fluffy. Beat in eggs
and vanilla. Beat in flour mixture alternately with sour cream, mixing
just until blended. Spoon half of batter into a buttered and floured
Bundt® pan. Spoon 2/3 of Walnut Filling over batter. Spread
remaining batter over filling; smooth top. Dot with remaining filling.
Bake at 350 degrees for 40 minutes, until a toothpick inserted near
center tests done. Cool cake in pan on a wire rack for 15 minutes.
Run a knife around pan sides to loosen; turn cake out onto a serving
platter. Serves 12.

Walnut Filling:

1/2 c. all-purpose flour
2 T. butter, softened
1 t. cinnamon

1-1/4 c. chopped walnuts
1/2 c. maple syrup

With a fork, mix together flour, butter and cinnamon in a small bowl
until crumbly. Stir in nuts and syrup.

*A vintage hand-cranked mini food chopper makes short
work of chopping nuts for cakes, cookies and other recipes.*

Farm-Fresh *Breakfasts*

Niles Coffee Cake

Dawn Wright
Marysville, OH

I had a dear elderly lady friend, Martha, who rented me a room when I was younger. She would make this most delicious coffee cake and we couldn't keep out of it. She always called it "Niles Coffee Cake" after the church she attended in Niles, Michigan. I loved her dearly and I always think of her when I make this coffee cake.

1 loaf frozen bread dough
1 c. chopped pecans or walnuts
1/2 c. cook & serve butterscotch
    pudding mix

1/2 c. butter
1/2 c. brown sugar, packed

The night before, let frozen bread dough stand at room temperature for one hour. Cut dough into 16 pieces and roll into balls. Spray a Bundt® pan with non-stick vegetable spray; sprinkle nuts into bottom of pan. Arrange dough balls in pan; sprinkle with pudding mix and set aside. In a small saucepan over medium-high heat, melt butter and brown sugar together. Pour hot mixture over dough balls. Cover pan; let rise overnight at room temperature. In the morning, bake at 325 degrees for 25 to 30 minutes, until rolls are light golden. Turn out onto a decorative plate; serve warm. Serves 6 to 8.

A weekend morning is the perfect time for an old-fashioned kaffeeklatsch to chat over coffee cake and coffee. Invite a girlfriend, or the new neighbor you've been wanting to get to know better, to share the latest news...you'll be so glad you did!

Mary Ann's Sunrise Egg Bake

Kathy Grashoff
Fort Wayne, IN

This is my absolute go-to egg casserole...it is so good! It's my mother-in-law's recipe and I have been using it for over 30 years. You should see my poor recipe card...you can tell it's a favorite! I always make a couple of all-vegetable bakes, too...try adding onions, colorful red and green peppers and whatever else you like.

1 doz. eggs, beaten
1 c. evaporated milk
2 t. dry mustard
salt and pepper to taste
8-oz. pkg. shredded Cheddar
   cheese

1 c. cooked ham, chopped
8-oz. can sliced mushrooms,
   drained
1/4 c. butter, diced

In a large bowl, whisk eggs, milk, mustard, salt and pepper together. Stir in cheese, ham and mushrooms. Pour into a lightly greased 13"x9" baking pan; dot with butter. Bake, uncovered, at 300 degrees for 45 minutes. Cool slightly before slicing into squares. Makes 12 servings.

Serve up individual portions of breakfast eggs in retro pressed-glass "hen-on-a-nest" dishes. The chicken-shaped lids will keep food hot and tasty, with a dash of fun added!

Farm-Fresh *Breakfasts*

Golden Hashbrown Casserole

Renae Scheiderer
Beallsville, OH

*A wonderful recipe to make when you have company coming...
just pop it in the oven and let it bake while you visit!*

6 eggs, beaten
12-oz. can evaporated milk
1 t. salt
1/2 t. pepper
30-oz. pkg. frozen shredded
   hashbrowns

8-oz. pkg. shredded Cheddar
   cheese
1 onion, chopped
1 green pepper, chopped
1 c. cooked ham, diced

Whisk eggs, milk, salt and pepper in a large bowl. Add remaining ingredients; mix well. Pour mixture into a greased 13"x9" baking pan. Bake, uncovered, at 350 degrees for 60 to 65 minutes, or until eggs are set. Makes 10 to 12 servings.

Make your own country-style sausage patties...it's simple. To one pound ground pork, add one teaspoon ground sage, 3/4 teaspoon salt, 3/4 teaspoon pepper and 1/4 teaspoon brown sugar. A dash or two of cayenne pepper can be added too. Blend well, form into four patties and brown in a skillet...delicious!

Custardy French Toast

Sarah Cameron
Maryville, TN

Absolutely the best French toast you'll ever eat!

6 eggs, beaten
3/4 c. whipping cream
3/4 c. milk
1/4 c. sugar
1/4 t. cinnamon

1 loaf French bread, thickly
  sliced
2 T. butter, divided
Optional: powdered sugar

In a large shallow bowl, whisk eggs, cream, milk, sugar and cinnamon until well blended. Dip bread slices one at a time into egg mixture, turning to allow both sides to absorb mixture. Melt one tablespoon butter on a non-stick griddle over medium heat. Cook for about 4 minutes per side, until golden and firm to the touch. Repeat with remaining butter and bread. Dust with powdered sugar, if desired. Serve with warm Cinnamon Syrup. Serves 6 to 8.

Cinnamon Syrup:

1 c. water
1 c. dark brown sugar, packed

2 T. whipping cream
1/2 t. cinnamon

Combine water and brown sugar in a heavy saucepan. Bring to a boil over high heat, stirring until sugar dissolves. Boil until syrup reduces to one cup, about 10 minutes. Remove from heat; whisk in cream and cinnamon. Serve warm. Syrup may be refrigerated, then rewarmed at serving time. Makes about 2 cups.

Keep tea towels handy on a peg rack...stitch a folded loop
of rick rack to one corner of the towels for hanging.

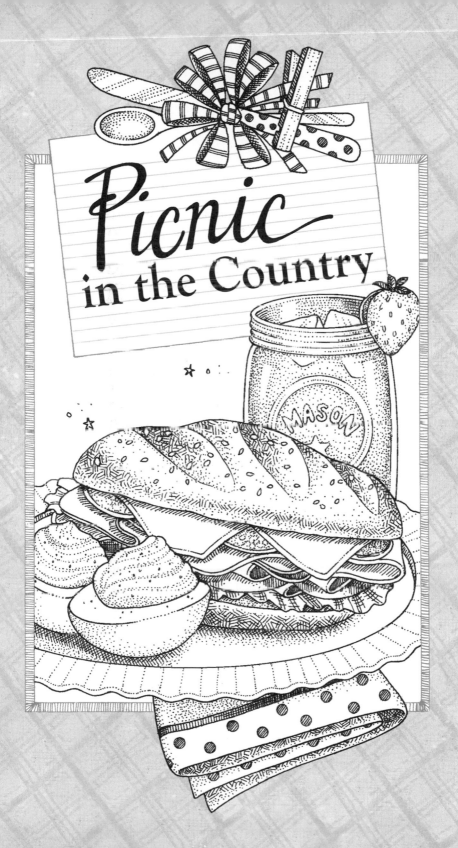

Picnic
in the Country

Hearty Hoagie

JoAnn
Gooseberry Patch

We love to grill these sandwiches practically year 'round in our backyard fire ring. You can also slide the foil-wrapped sandwich onto a baking sheet and bake it at 350 degrees until hot.

2 T. olive oil
1 T. white wine vinegar
1/3 c. fresh basil, chopped
1 loaf French bread, halved
   lengthwise

6-oz. pkg. sliced mozzarella
   cheese, divided
6-oz. pkg. sliced pastrami
2 roma tomatoes, thinly sliced
pepper to taste

Whisk together oil, vinegar and basil in a small bowl; set aside. Hollow out bottom half of loaf, leaving a 1/2-inch thick shell. Layer with half of cheese, all of the pastrami and tomatoes. Drizzle with oil mixture; sprinkle with pepper. Layer with remaining cheese; add top half of loaf. Wrap in aluminum foil. Grill over medium heat for 20 to 25 minutes, turning every 5 minutes, until heated through. Slice crosswise to serve. Makes 4 to 6 servings.

Fill an old wooden sugar bucket with crushed ice and bottles of soda pop...everyone can help themselves to a frosty beverage.

Picnic in the Country

Farmhands' Stuffed Sandwich

Barbara Shultis
South Egremont, MA

You'll love this oversized sandwich...wrapped in plastic, it's perfect for carrying to a picnic. I've done SO many tasty variations on this sandwich...chicken with barbecue sauce, ham & Swiss with coleslaw, corned beef & sauerkraut with Thousand Island dressing. The mix & match possibilities are endless!

1 round loaf hearty bread
2 T. Italian salad dressing
8 slices provolone cheese, divided
1/8 lb. deli salami, sliced
2-1/4 oz. can sliced black olives, drained
1/2 lb. mild Italian pork sausage links, browned and sliced

1 thick slice red onion
6 T. pizza sauce
6 pepperoncini, drained and sliced
1/4 lb. deli turkey, sliced
4-oz. jar sun-dried tomatoes in oil, drained and sliced
2 T. grated Parmesan cheese
Optional: 2 T. garlic, pressed

Slice off top quarter of loaf; hollow out top and bottom of loaf. Brush salad dressing inside bottom half. Layer with half of cheese slices; layer on remaining ingredients in order listed, ending with remaining cheese slices. Replace top half of loaf. Place on a baking sheet; set another baking sheet on top. Weight down with a heavy object like a food can or a cast-iron skillet. Let stand for 30 minutes to one hour. Cut into wedges to serve. Makes 10 servings.

Wicker picnic baskets just like Mom's are easy to find at tag sales... they bring back fond childhood memories of picnic fun! When yours isn't being used to tote picnic goodies, keep it in the kitchen to hold a collection of favorite cookbooks.

Egg Salad Sandwiches

Jenni Staroscik
Castle Rock, CO

Try replacing some of the onion with snipped fresh chives...delightful!

6 eggs, hard-boiled, peeled and
    coarsely chopped
1/2 c. shredded Cheddar cheese
1 onion, finely chopped
2/3 c. mayonnaise
1 t. mustard

1/4 t. paprika
1/4 t. celery salt
1/4 t. salt
1/4 t. pepper
8 slices bread, toasted

Mix all ingredients together except bread. Cover and refrigerate until serving time. Serve on toasted bread. Makes 4 sandwiches.

Mix up some herbal vinegar. Fill a Mason jar with a cup of finely chopped fresh herbs like parsley, chives, basil and dill. Pour in 2 cups white wine vinegar, heated just to boiling. Cap the jar and let steep, shaking it gently now and then. Strain the vinegar after 3 weeks and use it to jazz up salads and deli sandwiches.

Picnic in the Country

Picnic Salad Skewers

Pam James
Delaware, OH

What a fun way to pack a salad! For a meal-in-one version,
slide on some cubes of Cheddar cheese and cold cuts too.

8 new redskin potatoes
8 pearl onions
1 green pepper, cut into
   1-inch squares
1 red or yellow pepper, cut into
   1-inch squares

16 cherry tomatoes
1 zucchini, sliced 1/4-inch thick
8 wooden skewers
Optional: 4-oz. container
   crumbled feta cheese

Cover potatoes with water in a saucepan; bring to a boil over medium heat. Cook for 10 to 13 minutes, adding onions after 5 minutes; drain and cool. Thread vegetables alternately onto skewers. Arrange skewers in a large shallow plastic container. Drizzle with vinaigrette. Cover and refrigerate for at least one hour, turning frequently. Sprinkle with cheese before serving, if desired. Makes 8 servings.

Vinaigrette:

2/3 c. olive oil
1/3 c. red wine vinegar
2 cloves garlic, minced

1 T. dried oregano
1 t. salt
1/4 t. pepper

Whisk all ingredients together.

A rustic metal watering can
makes a charming centerpiece
filled with stems of cutting-garden
favorites like silver dollar plant,
Chinese lanterns and bells of Ireland.

Mom's Strawberry Lemonade

Kathleen Sturm
Corona, CA

*Here in southern California, we're lucky to have a lemon tree in
our backyard. This refreshing thirst quencher is a staple
in our fridge during the hot summer months.*

2 c. lemon juice
2 c. sugar

1 c. strawberries, hulled and
puréed

In a one-gallon jug or pitcher, combine lemon juice, sugar and puréed
strawberries. Mix to start dissolving sugar. Add enough water to fill
jug. Stir until sugar is dissolved completely. Chill; serve ice-cold.
Makes one gallon.

Homemade Root Beer

Beth Bundy
Long Prairie, MN

A tried & true recipe that will really take you back in time.

3/4 c. water
1/4 t. vanilla extract
1/2 c. sugar
1/4 c. honey

1/2 t. plus 1/8 t. root beer
concentrate
4-1/4 c. carbonated water or
club soda

Combine water and vanilla in a saucepan. Heat over low heat until
steaming. Remove from heat. Add sugar and honey; stir until
dissolved. Add concentrate. Mix well and cool in refrigerator. When
chilled, slowly add carbonated water or club soda. Serve immediately.
Makes about 6 servings.

When fate hands you a lemon, make lemonade.
– Dale Carnegie

Picnic in the Country

Pineapple Cheese Ball

Michelle Campen
Peoria, IL

Tote along one of these yummy cheese balls in a mini cooler with a box of crisp crackers to munch on after a hike in the country.

8-oz. pkg. cream cheese,
    softened
2 c. chopped pecans, divided
1/4 c. green pepper, chopped

8-oz. can crushed pineapple,
    drained
2 T. onion, chopped
1 T. seasoned salt

Beat cream cheese until smooth. Blend in one cup pecans and remaining ingredients. Shape into a ball; roll in remaining pecans. Wrap in plastic wrap. Refrigerate until ready to serve. Makes one cheese ball.

Box lunches are a fun way to serve up a picnic...indoors or out! Decorate shoeboxes with scrapbooking paper, stickers, ribbons and bows. Tuck a sandwich, a shiny red apple, some cookies and a napkin into each box.

Tuna & Egg Salad Sandwiches

Kimberly Stine
Milford, PA

Not your ordinary tuna salad sandwich! Only the egg whites are used...
chop the hard-cooked yolks to sprinkle over a salad.

2 6-oz. cans white tuna,
 drained and flaked
1/4 c. celery, minced
2 T. onion, minced
salt and pepper to taste
2 eggs, hard-boiled, peeled and
 halved

1/3 c. mayonnaise
8 slices Italian bread
Garnish: lettuce leaves, tomato
 slices, pickles

In a large bowl, combine tuna, celery, onion, salt and pepper to taste.
Chop egg whites and add to mixture, setting aside yolks for another
recipe. Mix well and add mayonnaise until desired consistency. Serve
on bread, garnished as desired with lettuce, tomatoes and pickles.
Makes 4 sandwiches.

The next time you see a roadside stand in the country,
stop and take a look! You're sure to find the freshest
fruits & veggies, cut flowers and even homemade
goodies like pickles, preserves, pies and cakes.

Picnic in the Country

Almost Heaven Chicken Salad

Pamela Breesawitz
White Sulphur Springs, WV

This chicken salad is a local favorite. My mother would often make it to take along on Sunday picnics as a light lunch. Even though she is no longer with us, I still make this recipe for my family...everyone loves it!

1/2 T. lemon juice
3 lbs. chicken breast, cooked
   and cubed
3/4 c. celery, finely diced

1/2 c. onion, finely chopped
1 c. mayonnaise
1 c. sour cream
salt and pepper to taste

Sprinkle lemon juice over chicken in a large bowl. Add remaining ingredients; mix well. Cover and chill well. May be served as a luncheon salad or on sandwiches. Makes 10 to 15 servings.

It's easy to tote a salad to a picnic. Mix it up in
a plastic zipping bag, seal and set it right in the cooler.
When you arrive at the picnic grounds, simply tip
the salad into a serving bowl.

Ham & Pickle Roll-Ups

Kristi Ohler
Rockwood, PA

When I take these roll-ups to a family get-together, they are gone before we even sit down to eat dinner! They are very tasty and so easy to make.

8-oz. pkg. cream cheese,
  softened
1 lb. deli ham, thinly sliced

32-oz. jar dill pickle spears,
  drained

Spread cream cheese on ham slices. Lay a pickle at the edge of each ham slice and roll up. Push a toothpick through it to hold it together. Slice into pieces the size you prefer. Store roll-ups in an airtight container; keep refrigerated. Makes 2 to 3 dozen.

Keep picnic food cold...fill plastic bottles with homemade lemonade or iced tea, freeze and tuck into your picnic cooler. As the bottles thaw, you'll have refreshing beverages to enjoy too.

Picnic in the Country

Horseradish Deviled Eggs

Karen McCann
Marion, OH

I remember when my mother first made these deviled eggs. She just chuckled as we tried to guess what was in them...horseradish! It gives the eggs a mild but zesty flavor.

6 eggs, hard-boiled, peeled and
   halved lengthwise
1/4 c. mayonnaise
1 to 2 T. prepared horseradish
1/4 t. mustard

1/8 t. salt
1/8 t. pepper
Optional: 1/2 t. dill weed
Garnish: paprika

Scoop egg yolks into a bowl. Arrange egg white halves on a platter and set aside. Mash yolks with a fork. Add mayonnaise, horseradish to taste, mustard, salt, pepper and dill weed, if using; mix well. Spoon mixture into egg whites; sprinkle with paprika. Refrigerate until ready to serve. Makes 12 servings.

Toting deviled eggs to a carry-in? Nestle the eggs in a bed of shredded lettuce or curly parsley to keep them from sliding around...they'll arrive looking scrumptious!

Chicken Noodle Burgers

Judy Borecky
Escondido, CA

This recipe is from my mother. She lived to see her great-great-grandchildren and her 100th birthday, bless her heart. Mother loved to cook and all 5 generations of our family love her noodle burgers!

1-1/4 lbs. ground beef round
10-3/4 oz. can chicken noodle
   soup, drained
1/3 c. instant oats, uncooked
1 egg, beaten
onion salt and pepper to taste
1/2 lb. sliced mushrooms

1/4 c. butter
3 T. all-purpose flour
1 c. chicken broth
1 c. half-and-half
1 t. Dijon mustard
salt and pepper to taste

Combine ground beef, soup, oats, egg, onion salt and pepper. Mix all until just blended and form into 6 patties. Place patties in a skillet over medium-high heat. Add a little water to the skillet so patties will steam as they fry. Meanwhile, make gravy in a separate skillet. Sauté mushrooms in butter until tender. Stir in flour, broth and half-and-half; cook until slightly thickened. Stir in mustard; add salt and pepper to taste. Serve gravy over noodle burgers. Makes 6 servings.

Hang a collection of fanciful
straw hats on a rack
by the kitchen door, just
waiting for a trip into
town or a few minutes
in the garden.

Picnic in the Country

Farm Sale Barbecue

Mardell Ross
Genoa, IL

These delicious sandwiches are a family tradition after we watch the parade at the local pumpkin festival.

2 lbs. ground beef
2 onions, chopped
10-3/4 oz. can tomato soup
3 T. catsup

1 T. dry mustard
1 T. vinegar
8 to 10 hamburger buns, split

In a large skillet over medium heat, brown ground beef and onions together; drain. Add soup, catsup, mustard and vinegar. Let simmer for 10 minutes or more. Serve spooned onto buns. Serves 8 to 10.

No picnic table? No problem! Lay a length of plywood (or even an old door) across a couple of sawhorses and toss on a checkered tablecloth. Add straw bales for seating and you're ready for a farm-style picnic!

Shrimp-Stuffed Tomato Poppers

Holly Curry
Grahamsville, NY

A recipe given to me at a church supper...it is so very good!
Use a tiny measuring spoon to scoop out the tomatoes.

2 pts. cherry tomatoes
1/2 lb. cooked shrimp, peeled
   and finely chopped
8-oz. pkg. light cream cheese,
   softened
1/4 c. light mayonnaise

1/4 c. grated Parmesan cheese
1 t. prepared horseradish
1 t. lemon juice
salt and pepper to taste
Garnish: chopped fresh parsley

Cut a thin slice off the top of each tomato; scoop out and discard
pulp. Place tomatoes upside-down on a paper towel; let drain for
30 minutes. Combine remaining ingredients except parsley; blend
until smooth. Spoon into tomatoes; sprinkle with parsley. Serves 16.

Brightly colored bandannas are fun to use as super-sized
napkins. Keep a stack of them on hand and you'll be
ready for a picnic or casual get-together anytime.

Picnic in the Country

Mini Bacon-Cheese Balls

Ruby Dorosh
Shippensburg, PA

These tasty bite-size appetizers are sure to be a hit at your next picnic, potluck or pitch-in dinner!

8-oz. container chive & onion
  cream cheese spread,
  softened
8-oz. pkg. shredded mozzarella
  cheese
4 slices bacon, crisply cooked
  and crumbled

1/2 t. Italian seasoning
1/2 t. garlic powder
1/2 c. walnuts, toasted and
  ground or finely chopped

Mix cheeses until well blended; stir in bacon and seasonings. Shape mixture into balls by level teaspoonfuls. Roll each ball in walnuts. Place in a serving dish; cover with plastic wrap. Refrigerate at least 2 hours before serving. Makes about 4-1/2 dozen.

A fluffy chenille bedspread that has become a little shabby is just right for a picnic spread. Tuck one in your car and you'll be ready for picnicking at a moment's notice.

Wiener Kabobs

Clarie Bertram
Lexington, KY

My brother & I always felt so grown-up when Mom served these appetizers. Of course we had to take off the olives and stick them on our fingers...maybe that's why we liked them so much!

1-lb. pkg. mini cocktail wieners
11-oz. can pineapple chunks,
    drained
5-oz. jar green olives with
    pimentos, drained

1/2 lb. favorite cheese, cubed
party picks or mini wooden
    skewers

Place one wiener, one pineapple chunk, one olive and one cheese cube on each pick or skewer. Repeat until ingredients are used up. Arrange picks on a serving plate and cover with plastic wrap. Keep chilled until ready to serve. Makes 2 to 3 dozen.

Retro plastic catsup & mustard squeeze bottles
add a little fun to any meal.

Picnic in the Country

Corn Relish Dip

Dianne Young
South Jordan, UT

This is a real crowd-pleaser...everyone always asks for the recipe.
Serve with tortilla chips for dipping or spoon into lettuce cups
and serve as a salad. Either way, it's yummy!

3 roma tomatoes, diced
2 avocados, pitted, peeled and
   diced
15-oz. can shoepeg corn,
   drained
16-oz. can black beans, drained
   and rinsed

3.8-oz. can sliced black olives,
   drained
1/4 to 1/2 c. onion, diced
16-oz. bottle zesty Italian salad
   dressing

Combine all vegetables in a large salad bowl; toss to mix. Add
dressing to taste, a little at a time. Keep chilled; stir again before
serving. Makes 8 servings.

Keep tea towels at your fingertips on the counter by the
kitchen sink. Slip rolled-up towels into a
vintage milk bottle carrier.

Aunt Janie's Famous Cheese Ball

Wendy O'Hara-Reaume
Ontario, Canada

This recipe has been a part of our family gatherings for as long as I can remember. With its savory combination of flavors, it's always a big hit at parties...maybe you'd better double the recipe!

2 8-oz. pkgs. cream cheese, softened
4-oz. container crumbled blue cheese
1 c. shredded Cheddar cheese
1 green pepper, diced
2-oz. jar diced pimentos, drained

1 t. Worcestershire sauce
1 t. garlic powder
1 c. sliced almonds
round buttery crackers or club crackers

Combine all ingredients except almonds and crackers; blend well. Form into one or two balls. Place almonds into a lidded plastic container. Place cheese ball into container (one at a time, if making two) and cover with lid. Shake vigorously to coat with nuts. Wrap and refrigerate until serving time. Serve with crackers. Makes 10 to 12 servings.

Show off a collection of favorite stoneware mixing bowls on open-front kitchen shelves. Add a pretty shelf edging of scrapbooking paper, trimmed with decorative-edge scissors.

Picnic in the Country

Nutty Olive Spread

Hope Davenport
Portland, TX

Tuck a jar of this creamy spread, a cheese spreader and some crisp crackers into a basket for a neighborly gift that's sure to be welcome.

2 3-oz. pkgs. cream cheese, softened
1/2 c. mayonnaise
5-3/4 oz. jar green olives with pimentos, drained and finely chopped

1/2 c. pecans, toasted and finely chopped
1/8 t. pepper
assorted crackers

In a large bowl, beat cream cheese until fluffy; beat in mayonnaise. Stir in olives, pecans and pepper. Cover and chill overnight. Serve with crackers. Makes about 2 cups.

Keep the fridge sweet-smelling...tuck in a cotton ball that has been moistened with vanilla extract. A little trick that works with picnic coolers too.

Raspberry Punch

Rosie Jones
Wabash, IN

For toasting a festive occasion, replace the cider
with sparkling white wine.

2 c. apple cider
3 c. cranberry-raspberry
  juice cocktail
1 qt. lemonade

Optional: 1 lemon, thinly sliced,
  fresh mint leaves,
  fresh raspberries

Combine apple cider, cranberry-raspberry juice and lemonade in a
large pitcher or punch bowl. If desired, garnish glasses with lemon
slices, fresh mint leaves or raspberries. Makes 8 servings.

Keep buzzing bees out of picnic beverages. Just stitch 4 large
buttons from Grandma's button box to a large doily and
drape it over an open pitcher...it's that easy!

Picnic in the Country

Summary Sparkle

Eleanor Bamford
Boonton, NJ

Serve in tall fluted glasses with plenty of ice...oh-so refreshing!

48-oz. bottle ruby red
   grapefruit juice
12-oz. can frozen orange juice
   concentrate, thawed
6-oz. can frozen lemonade
   concentrate, thawed

2-ltr. bottle lemon-lime soda,
   chilled
Optional: lemon slices, fresh
   mint sprigs

In a one-gallon pitcher, stir together all juices; cover and refrigerate until chilled. At serving time, add soda; garnish as desired. Serve immediately. Makes 16 to 20 servings.

A sweet vintage-style clothespin bag makes a handy
wall holder for recipe cards or mail.

Country Bologna Salad

Karen Smyers
Yadkinville, NC

This is my mother's recipe...it was handed down from her mother, my Grandmother Startzell, so it is quite old. The hard-boiled eggs are my own addition.

3 lbs. beef bologna, coarsely
    chopped
16-oz. jar sweet pickles, drained
2 eggs, hard-boiled, peeled and
    chopped

1 to 1-1/2 c. mayonnaise-style
    salad dressing

Grind bologna and pickles in a food grinder to desired medium to coarse texture. Transfer to a large bowl; add eggs. Stir in salad dressing to desired consistency. Blend ingredients together. Spread on bread for sandwiches or on crackers for appetizers. Makes 15 to 20 servings.

An old-fashioned food grinder is easy to clean when you've finished using it. Just put a half-slice of bread through the grinder as the last item...the bread will remove any food residue.

Picnic in the Country

Picnic Pinwheels

Kimberly Hancock
Murrieta, CA

These roll-ups are lots of fun for kids, and moms as well, because they can be made in just minutes. It's a great spin on our old standby, the peanut butter & jelly sandwich. Crunchy apple can be substituted for the banana too. Yummy!

1/3 c. creamy peanut butter
4 8-inch flour tortillas

1 c. banana, chopped
1/4 c. low-fat granola cereal

Spread peanut butter on each tortilla; top with banana and granola. Tightly roll up tortillas and cut each one in half. Wrap roll-ups in plastic wrap or aluminum foil to pack in lunchboxes. Serves 4.

Instead of one large picnic basket, why not pack individual lunches for everyone in children's sand pails? Line the pails with checked napkins and tie a name tag to the handle of each pail.

Spicy Cheese Crispies

Molly Wilson
Box Elder, SD

All the kids loved the regular mild-flavored cheese crispies and my uncle told Mama she should make some for the adults...so she did!

1 c. margarine, softened
8-oz. pkg. shredded sharp
   Cheddar cheese
2 c. all-purpose flour

1 t. cayenne pepper
1/2 t. salt
2 c. crispy rice cereal
Optional: 1 c. pecan halves

In a large bowl, blend together margarine and cheese. Add flour, cayenne pepper and salt; stir in cereal. Shape into small balls and place on ungreased baking sheets. Flatten each ball with a fork. Top each with a pecan half, if desired. Bake at 300 degrees for 20 minutes. Cool; store tightly covered. Makes about 6 dozen.

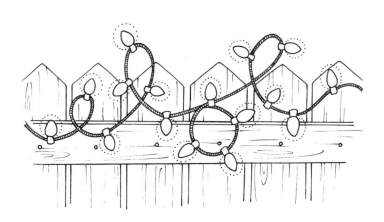

Wind sparkling yellow or white lights along the garden fence and in the trees for a twinkling firefly effect as the sun sets.

Picnic in the Country

Tasty Taco Roll-Ups

Kelly Bartle-Gardner
Central Square, NY

*Sprinkle on some finely chopped red and green pepper
for extra color and crunchiness.*

3 8-oz. pkgs. cream cheese
1/2 c. shredded Cheddar cheese
1 1/4 oz. pkg. taco seasoning
  mix

10 to 12 10-inch flour tortillas
Garnish: salsa

Stir together cheeses and seasoning mix until well blended. Spread evenly onto tortillas; roll up tightly. Cut rolls into bite-size pieces; chill. Serve with salsa for dipping. Makes about 5 to 6 dozen.

Vintage tin pie plates are practical for holding picnic dinners... not flimsy like paper plates! Look for tins that are stamped with the names of the original bakeries.

Sour Cream Dill Dip

Frankie Barnette
Colonial Heights, VA

This dip recipe brings back so many memories of my grandmother! My brother and I were always asking our "Gaga" to make it for us when we were little. We just loved eating it with ruffled potato chips or toasted bread pieces. Now that she has passed on, I'm the one who always makes this great dip.

1 c. sour cream
2/3 c. mayonnaise
1-1/2 t. dill weed

1 t. seasoning salt
1 t. dried, minced onion
potato chips, cut-up veggies

Mix all ingredients together except potato chips and vegetables. Cover and refrigerate for one to 2 hours, until dip becomes firm. Serve with chips and vegetables for dipping. Makes 12 to 15 servings.

Baby carrots, celery stalks, cherry tomatoes and broccoli flowerets are all tasty dippers...why not try something new with your next bowl of dip? Slices of yellow summer squash, romaine lettuce leaves and even lightly steamed green beans, snow peas and asparagus spears are crunchy and full of flavor.

Picnic in the Country

Cheesy Bean Dip

Diana Seiler
Goddard, KS

*This dip is a favorite at our family get-togethers like picnics,
football games or just Sunday night gatherings.*

2 16-oz. cans refried beans
2 8-oz. pkgs. cream cheese,
   softened
Garnish: shredded Cheddar or
   Swiss cheese, chopped green
   onions

tortilla chips, snack crackers

Spoon beans into a large bowl. Slowly blend in cream cheese until
creamy, using an electric mixer set on medium-low speed. Garnish as
desired with cheese and onions. Chill before serving with chips or
crackers. Serves 6 to 8.

Primitive-style wooden cutting boards in fun shapes like pigs,
fish or roosters can often be found at tag sales. Put them
to use as whimsical party snack servers.

Zesty Tortilla Roll-Ups

Rosemary Vorndran
Diamond Bar, CA

We always share several kinds of finger foods like these roll-ups before the main meal at family get-togethers. It gives us a chance to mingle, chat and catch up with each other.

2 8-oz. pkgs. cream cheese, softened
2 4-oz. cans chopped green chiles, drained

2 to 3 T. milk
10 to 12 burrito-size flour tortillas

In a medium bowl, mix cream cheese and chiles with enough milk to make smooth and easy to spread. Spread mixture on tortillas and roll up tightly. Slice rolled-up tortillas in one-inch pieces and arrange on a serving plate. May be made the day before, chilled and sliced when ready to serve. Makes about 1-1/2 dozen.

Straw shopping totes from the thrift store make whimsical planters for marigolds and zinnias...just slip them over fence posts and fill with flowers.

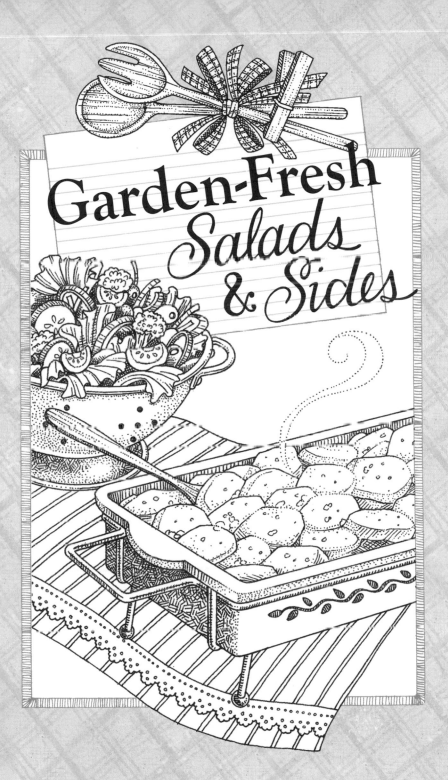

Garden-Fresh
Salads
& Sides

Garden-Fresh Green Beans

Vickie Fallis
Osgood, IN

This recipe came from a cookbook from the 1940's. It's such a treat made with the first green beans, peppers and tomatoes of the season.

4 to 6 slices smoked bacon,
    diced
2 lbs. green beans, trimmed
1 onion, diced

1 green pepper, diced
1 tomato, diced
salt and pepper to taste

In a large heavy skillet over medium heat, cook bacon until crisp. Set aside bacon, reserving drippings in skillet. Add remaining ingredients to skillet. Cover tightly and reduce heat; cook for 10 minutes. Add just enough water to cover bottom of skillet; increase heat and cook until beans are tender. Stir in cooked bacon. Serves 8.

I have friends in overalls whose friendship I would not swap
for the favor of the kings of the world.
-Thomas Edison

Garden-Fresh Salads & Sides

Creamy Country Corn

Sharon Demers
Dolores, CO

*This easy recipe is a tasty accompaniment to
grilled meat and a crisp green tossed salad.*

6 green onions, chopped
3 T. butter
16-oz. pkg. frozen corn, thawed
2 t. cornstarch
1/2 c. half-and-half

1/4 c. water
1/2 t. salt
1/4 to 1/2 t. pepper
1 c. cherry tomatoes, halved

In a skillet over medium heat, sauté onions in butter until tender,
about 2 to 3 minutes. Stir in corn; cover and cook until heated
through, about 4 to 5 minutes. In a small bowl, combine cornstarch,
half-and-half, water, salt and pepper; whisk until smooth. Stir into
corn mixture. Bring to a boil. Cook, uncovered, until thickened, about
2 minutes. Stir in tomatoes. Makes 6 servings.

Make tangy green tomato pickles with the last of the garden's
tomatoes...it's so easy! Quarter the tomatoes and drop them
into a jar of leftover dill pickle juice. Return the jar to
the icebox for a few days before enjoying.

Cow-Country Beans

Debra Crisp
Merlin, OR

My family especially likes this recipe served over potato pancakes.

3 c. dried red beans
1 lb. cooked ham, cubed
1 onion, sliced
1 c. celery, diced
8-oz. can tomato sauce
2 T. bacon bits

2 T. chili powder
1 T. brown sugar, packed
2 t. garlic powder
1/2 t. smoke-flavored cooking
  sauce
1/2 t. salt

Cover dried beans with water in a bowl; soak overnight. In the morning, drain beans. Combine with remaining ingredients in a slow cooker. Cover and cook on high setting for 8 to 10 hours. Makes 8 to 10 servings.

No more boring drawer knobs! Glue on retro-style metal bottle caps...they're easy to find at flea markets and craft stores.

Amish Macaroni Salad

Diana Strawbridge
Ashtabula, OH

This macaroni salad is the best we've ever had! My aunt gave me the recipe...she lived near an Amish community in Ohio for many years and her Amish neighbor shared this with her.

8-oz. pkg. elbow macaroni,
    uncooked and divided
4 eggs, hard-boiled, peeled and
    chopped
1 onion, chopped
3 stalks celery, chopped
1 red pepper, chopped
1-1/2 c. mayonnaise-type salad
    dressing

3 T. mustard
2 T. dill pickle relish
1/2 c. sugar
2-1/4 t. white vinegar
3/4 t. celery seed
1/4 t. salt

Measure out 2 cups macaroni, reserving the rest for another recipe. Bring a pot of salted water to a boil. Add macaroni to pot and cook for 8 to 10 minutes, until tender. Drain and rinse with cool water. In a large bowl, stir together eggs and vegetables. In a small bowl, stir together remaining ingredients and pour over egg mixture. Stir in macaroni until well blended. Cover and chill for 2 hours to overnight before serving. Serves 8.

For a whimsical recipe card holder, hot-glue a clip clothespin to the handle of a tag-sale potato masher.

Creamy Bacon & Herb Succotash

Vickie
Gooseberry Patch

You'll love this deluxe version of an old harvest-time favorite...I do!

1/4 lb. bacon, chopped
1 onion, diced
10-oz. pkg. frozen lima beans
1/2 c. water
salt and pepper to taste

10-oz. pkg. frozen corn
1/2 c. whipping cream
1-1/2 t. fresh thyme, minced
Garnish: 2 t. fresh chives,
   snipped

In a Dutch oven over medium-high heat, cook bacon until crisp. Remove bacon, reserving 2 tablespoons drippings in Dutch oven. Add onion; sauté until tender, about 5 minutes. Add beans, water, salt and pepper; bring to a boil. Reduce heat; cover and simmer for 5 minutes. Stir in corn, cream and thyme; return to a simmer. Cook until vegetables are tender, about 5 minutes. Toss with reserved bacon and chives before serving. Makes 6 servings.

A wheelbarrow makes a convenient planter for
potted herbs...it's so easy to wheel to the kitchen door
and snip off sprigs for cooking.

Garden-Fresh Salads & Sides

Grandpa Jim's Potatoes

JoAnn Houghtby
Farmington, MN

After my grandma passed away, my grandpa learned to make coffee and cook for himself. It was just so adorable to see this 80-year-old man learning these skills for himself. This is a recipe that he was especially proud of...and it is SO good! He made it for our church potluck and it was a hit. I was so happy to go with him and see the twinkle in his eye.

8 to 10 potatoes, peeled, cooked and mashed
12-oz. pkg. bacon, crisply cooked and crumbled
8-oz. pkg. shredded Cheddar cheese
1-1/4 c. ranch salad dressing

Mix all ingredients together and spoon into a lightly greased 13"x9" baking pan. Bake, uncovered, at 375 degrees for 30 minutes, until heated through. Makes 12 to 15 servings.

A discarded window frame makes a memorable picture frame. Simply polish the panes with glass cleaner and place favorite photographs behind the openings. So sweet!

Good-for-You Southern Greens

Aubrey Dunne
Piscataway, NJ

On a wonderful trip down to North Carolina, our friends took us for authentic eastern North Carolina barbecue. We had some of the most delicious food we'd ever eaten. My husband loved the southern collard greens, but not all the fat they were cooked with. This recipe is my effort to make them a bit more healthy, but still serve up that down-home country flavor.

1/2 c. cooked ham, finely
   chopped
1/2 c. onion, finely chopped
1 bunch kale, trimmed

1/2 c. chicken broth
1/8 t. salt
1/8 t. pepper
Garnish: red wine vinegar

In a large skillet over medium heat, cook ham until slightly browned. Add remaining ingredients except vinegar. Cover; simmer for 15 minutes, or until kale turns soft and dark. Drizzle with vinegar to taste. Serves 4 to 6.

Sew up a quick shopping tote with snips of vintage fabrics like barkcloth and farmhouse calicos. It'll be so handy for carrying home goodies from the farmers' market!

Garden-Fresh Salads & Sides

Sweet-and-Sour Turnips

Barbara Ferree
New Freedom, PA

This Pennsylvania Dutch dish has been around for generations. We serve a community dinner at our church every year and I am always asked to bring my Sweet-and-Sour Turnips. I like them served with mashed potatoes.

5 to 6 turnips, peeled and sliced
   1/4-inch thick
salt to taste
1 egg, beaten

1/2 c. vinegar
1 c. sugar
1 T. all-purpose flour

Cover turnips with water in a large kettle; add salt as desired. Boil over medium-high heat until soft. Drain turnips thoroughly and return to kettle. Mix together egg, vinegar, sugar and flour until well blended. Add mixture to turnips and bring to a boil, stirring continuously to prevent scorching. Boil for approximately one minute; mixture will thicken slightly. Serves 4 to 6.

Create the perfect farmhouse porch with auction or tag-sale finds. Nothing says "country" like a porch swing and whitewashed wicker chairs...toss on pillows covered with vintage-print feedsacks.

Chopped Salad

JoEllen Ferington
Fountain Hills, AZ

*Serve alongside grilled sirloin or hamburgers and fresh-picked
ears of sweet corn...scrumptious!*

2 tomatoes, coarsely chopped
1/3 c. mayonnaise
1/2 t. salt
pepper to taste

1/4 t. cayenne pepper
1 head iceberg lettuce, chopped
6 thick slices bacon, crisply
   cooked and crumbled

Place tomatoes in a salad serving bowl; toss with mayonnaise and
seasonings. Cover and chill for 30 minutes to several hours. At
serving time, add lettuce and bacon to bowl. Stir to coat evenly.
Serves 4.

For a fresh change from spinach, give Swiss chard a try.
An old-timey favorite that probably grew in your
grandmother's garden, it's easy to serve too...just steam
until tender, then drizzle with cider vinegar to taste.

Garden-Fresh *Salads & Sides*

Cabbage Tomato Slaw

Tamara Parlor
Jacksonville, NC

This simple slaw tastes even better the next day!

1 head cabbage, chopped
1 sweet onion, chopped
2 tomatoes, diced

1/2 c. mayonnaise
salt and pepper to taste

Combine all ingredients in a large salad bowl. Toss to mix; cover and chill until serving time. Makes 6 servings.

There are always lots of yummy sides on the farmhouse table. If you have a small family, or if there's just the two of you at home, pick up a vintage divided serving dish or two...they're just right for serving up lots of sides without crowding the table.

Creamy Cabbage Bake

Kimberly Burditt
Summerville, SC

This recipe is a favorite at our family cookouts...real comfort food.

1 head cabbage, coarsely
    chopped
1 c. carrots, peeled and chopped
1 c. onion, chopped
10-3/4 oz. can cream of
    mushroom soup
1/2 c. plus 2 T. milk

1/2 t. seasoned salt
1 t. dried parsley
8-oz. pkg. shredded Swiss
    cheese
8-oz. pkg. shredded Parmesan
    cheese

Boil cabbage, carrots and onion in water till tender; drain. Combine with remaining ingredients. Put into a greased 13"x9" baking pan. Bake, uncovered, at 350 degrees for 45 minutes. Serves 12.

Seasoned Summer Squash

Debbie Jurczyk
Gilbertville, MA

So simple and so delicious! Our family never tires of this recipe when summer squash is in season.

1 cube beef bouillon
4 to 6 yellow squash, sliced
    1/4-inch thick

1 onion, sliced 1/4-inch thick
Garnish: butter, seasoned salt,
    pepper

Place bouillon cube and one inch water in a medium saucepan. Layer squash and onion slices in pan. Cover; bring to a boil over medium-high heat. Reduce to medium heat; boil gently until tender, 5 to 8 minutes. Drain well. Serve in individual bowls as a side, allowing each person to add butter, salt and pepper to taste. Serves 6.

Whip up a quick & easy valance for a kitchen window...
just drape several flowered tea towels over the curtain rod.

Scalloped Zucchini

Liz Gatewood
Madison, IN

*We own a farm and raise veggies so we always have plenty of zucchini.
I have come up with different ways to cook it and my family loves this
recipe. Choose small and medium zucchini...they're more tender than
the really big ones.*

4 to 5 zucchini, sliced
1 onion, sliced
2 c. pasteurized process cheese
   spread, sliced

1 sleeve rectangular buttery
   crackers, crushed
1/2 c. butter, sliced

Layer half each of zucchini, onion and cheese slices in a buttered
13"x9" baking pan. Repeat layering. Top with crackers and dot with
butter. Bake, uncovered, at 325 degrees until tender, about
40 minutes. Serves 8 to 10.

Look for heirloom fruits & vegetables at farmers' markets...
varieties that Grandma & Grandpa may have grown in
their garden. These fruits and veggies don't always look
picture-perfect but their flavor can't be beat.

Mixed-Up Pasta Salad

Kathy Doty
Dover, DE

A great recipe for large get-togethers...everyone loves this! You can use any combination of pasta shells, wheels, twists and tubes.

12-oz. pkg. tri-color mixed
    pasta shapes, uncooked
14-1/2 oz. can green beans,
    drained
14-1/2 oz. can wax beans,
    drained
14-1/2 oz. can kidney beans,
    drained and rinsed

1 c. sweet onion, chopped
1/2 c. olive oil
3/4 c. cider vinegar
2/3 c. sugar
Optional: 1/2 c. cherry
    tomatoes, halved
salt and pepper to taste

Cook pasta according to package directions; drain and rinse with cold water. Meanwhile, combine beans and onion in a large bowl; set aside. In a separate bowl, combine oil and vinegar; slowly add sugar and stir until dissolved. Add pasta, tomatoes and oil mixture to bean mixture. Sprinkle with salt and pepper. Toss gently; serve immediately or refrigerate until serving time. Serves 10 to 12.

Keep a ball of kitchen string right where you need it!
Simply drop it into a small teapot and pull out the
end of the string through the spout.

Garden-Fresh *Salads & Sides*

Red Pickled Eggs & Beets

Jane Brediger
Massillon, OH

This recipe was my mother's. It is now on the third generation.
My 4-year-old grandson calls them "pink eggs" and just
loves them! I make them in a half-gallon ice tea jar.

8 eggs, hard-boiled and peeled
1 sweet onion, thinly sliced
2 15-oz. cans small red beets,
   drained and juice reserved
1-1/2 c. cider vinegar
1-1/2 c. sugar

Place eggs in a large glass jar. Top with onion and beets; set aside.
Measure reserved beet juice and pour into a saucepan. Add equal
parts of vinegar and sugar (for example: to one cup beet juice, add
cup sugar and one cup vinegar). Bring just to a boil; stir to dissolve
sugar. Let cool for 5 minutes. Pour over eggs and beets, filling jar to
top. Cover; refrigerate for at least 2 days before serving. Makes
8 servings.

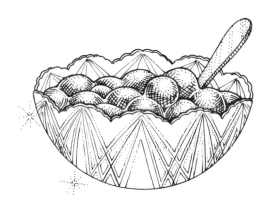

An antique cut-glass serving dish really shows off the sparkling
color of ruby red beets, bright green bread & butter pickles,
sunny apricot jam and other homemade preserves.

Bacon & Onion Mashed Potatoes

Sue Waldman
Chicago, IL

Gram and Mom used to fix mashed potatoes this delicious way...
I thought everybody did! Then I found out they did not, so why
not share. This is a good side dish with smoked meat or pork chops.

4 potatoes, peeled and quartered
3 slices bacon, chopped

2 c. green onions, green tops
only, sliced

Cover potatoes with water in a medium saucepan; boil until tender. When potatoes are cooked, drain, leaving potatoes in pan. Place pan back over low heat, shaking slightly to allow potatoes to dry. Remove from heat again; mash potatoes and set aside. Fry bacon in a skillet until crisp. Turn heat down to low; do not drain. Add onions, stirring to coat all. Add potatoes, mashing to blend in bacon, drippings and onions. Makes 4 servings.

Frame cherished handwritten recipes to hang in the kitchen.
They'll bring back sweet memories and will always
be nearby when you want to prepare them.

Garden-Fresh *Salads & Sides*

Cornbread Sage Dressing

Rosanna Dyck
Lime Springs, IA

This dressing comes from the heart of Dixie, where we used to live in Georgia and where we learned to love southern foods. Now that we live in Iowa, it is still our favorite with roast turkey.

13"x9" baking pan cornbread, crumbled
9 slices day-old white bread, torn

5 c. chicken broth or milk
1 T. dried sage
1/2 T. salt

Combine all ingredients in a very large bowl; toss together lightly. Spoon into a slow cooker. Cover and cook on low setting for about 3 hours. Makes 12 to 15 servings.

Homemade Cornbread:

3 eggs, beaten
1/2 c. water
1/2 c. margarine, melted
1 c. milk

1/2 c. onion, chopped
3/4 c. celery, chopped
1-1/2 c. self-rising cornmeal

Beat eggs and water; add remaining ingredients and mix well. Pour batter into a greased 13"x9" baking pan. Bake at 400 degrees for 30 minutes, until set and golden. Let cool.

A farmhouse kitchen favorite...knitted cotton dishcloths are a quick & easy project, even for beginning knitters. Why not give it a try?

Cheesy Spinach Baked Ziti

Lori Ritchey
Denver, PA

When I serve this tasty dish, everyone is happy to eat their spinach!

12-oz. pkg. ziti pasta, cooked
14-1/2 oz. can diced tomatoes
   with Italian herbs
9-oz. pkg. frozen creamed
   spinach, thawed

8-oz. pkg. grated Romano
   cheese
8-oz. pkg. shredded mozzarella
   cheese

Mix all ingredients except mozzarella cheese; spread in a greased 13"x9" baking pan. Top with mozzarella cheese. Cover and bake at 350 degrees for 30 minutes, until hot and bubbly. Serves 4.

Add a little sugar when boiling corn on the cob or simmering homemade tomato sauce. It brings out the natural sweetness and reduces any bitterness. Just a pinch will do!

Garden-Fresh Salads & Sides

Gnocchi & Vegetable Toss

Jennifer Patrick
Delaware, OH

This mixture of tender little potato dumplings and colorful veggies is almost a meal in itself.

17-1/2 oz. pkg. potato gnocchi,
   uncooked
1 lb. asparagus, cut into
   bite-size pieces
1 zucchini, halved and sliced
1 yellow squash, halved and
   sliced

10-oz. pkg. grape tomatoes,
   halved
10-oz. jar sun-dried tomato-
   basil pesto sauce
1/2 c. sour cream

In a stockpot, bring 4 quarts of water to a boil. Add gnocchi and vegetables. Return to a boil; boil for 2 to 3 minutes, until gnocchi floats to top; drain. Mix pesto sauce with sour cream. Add to gnocchi mixture; toss until coated thoroughly. Serve hot or cold. Makes 4 to 6 servings.

Snap up oversized letters at flea markets to spell out whimsical words...like EAT on a dining room wall or GROW on a garden fence!

German Hot Potato Salad

Jennifer Savino
Joliet, IL

*My grandma was famous for this recipe...she'd bring a huge bowl
to share at every family or community occasion.
Definitely a comfort food and so delicious!*

6 slices bacon, finely chopped
1 onion, sliced
1/3 c. vinegar
1/2 c. water
2 t. all-purpose flour
1 T. sugar

1-1/2 t. salt
1/4 t. pepper
1/2 c. fresh parsley, chopped
1-1/4 lbs. potatoes, peeled,
  sliced and cooked

In a large skillet, sauté bacon until crisp. Drain off most of drippings;
add onion and sauté for 2 minutes. Add remaining ingredients except
potatoes; cook and stir until thickened. Add potatoes and stir well.
Serve warm. Makes 4 to 6 servings.

Vintage days-of-the-week towels make such sweet
window toppers...just attach clip-on curtain rings.

Green Bean Bundles

Wendy Sensing
Brentwood, TN

Easy and delicious! This is one of our favorite side dishes to bring to church get-togethers. The dish always comes home empty and someone always wants the recipe, especially the garlic lovers.

3 14-1/2 oz. cans whole green
   beans, drained
8 slices bacon, cut in half
   crosswise

6 T. butter, melted
1/2 c. brown sugar, packed
2 to 3 cloves garlic, minced

Gather beans in bundles of 10; wrap each bundle with a half-slice of bacon. Arrange bundles in a lightly greased 13"x9" baking pan. Mix melted butter, sugar and garlic in small bowl; spoon over bundles. Cover and bake at 375 degrees for 30 minutes. Uncover; bake an additional 15 minutes. Serves 6.

Turn leftover mashed potatoes into twice-baked potatoes.
Stir in minced onion, crumbled bacon and shredded cheese
to taste and pat into individual ramekins. Bake at
350 degrees until hot and golden...delicious!

Broccoli-Cauliflower Salad

Janice Tarter
Morrow, OH

We grow our own vegetables on our country farm, so I'm always looking for new ways to serve fresh veggies. This is a very refreshing salad...great to make ahead and take to a picnic. It's very easy and very yummy!

1 head broccoli, chopped
1 head cauliflower, chopped
1 c. green onions, chopped
1/2 lb. bacon, crisply cooked
   and crumbled

1 c. mayonnaise-type salad
   dressing
1/2 c. sugar

Combine broccoli, cauliflower, onions and bacon in a large salad bowl. Mix dressing and sugar in a separate bowl. Drizzle over broccoli mixture; toss all together. Serve immediately or refrigerate until serving time. Serves 6 to 8.

A well-used wooden salad bowl is a terrific thrift-shop find. To restore the bowl's glowing finish, sand lightly inside and out with fine sandpaper. Rub a little vegetable oil over the bowl and let stand overnight, then wipe off any excess oil in the morning. It will be good as new!

Garden-Fresh *Salads & Sides*

Teresa's Easy-Peasy Salad

Teresa Ponder
Deland, FL

This salad was always served at holiday dinners year 'round when I was growing up...everyone liked the crunchy textures and the slightly sweet dressing. Now I make it for the holidays for my own family and for potlucks at work or church.

1 head lettuce, shredded
3 to 4 stalks celery, chopped
16-oz. pkg. frozen peas, cooked
   and cooled

1 lb. bacon, crisply cooked and
   crumbled

Place lettuce in a large salad bowl; layer with celery, peas and bacon. Serve with Special Dressing on the side, or pour dressing over salad at serving time. Keep refrigerated. Serves 6 to 8.

Special Dressing:

1-1/2 c. mayonnaise-type salad
   dressing

1/4 c. sugar
1 to 2 T. milk, divided

Mix together salad dressing and sugar. Add milk, one tablespoon at a time, until desired consistency is reached.

A whimsical kitchen decoration...vintage fruit crate labels from the 1930's and 1940's were always decorated with such fun designs. Look for them at flea markets or barn sales.

Mary's Baked Macaroni

Paula Weaver
Steeleville, IL

My mother's recipe for special dinners and company.

8-oz. pkg. elbow macaroni,
   uncooked and divided
1-1/2 c. milk
2 T. cornstarch
1/3 c. water
1-1/2 c. Colby Longhorn cheese,
   diced

3 eggs, beaten
1/2 c. oil
1 onion, diced
1/2 green pepper, diced
8-oz. can sliced mushrooms,
   drained
1 to 2 c. soda crackers, crushed

Measure out 1-1/2 cups macaroni, reserving the rest for another recipe. Cook macaroni according to package directions; drain. Heat milk, without bringing to a boil, in a saucepan over medium heat. In a small bowl, whisk together cornstarch and water; slowly stir into warmed milk. Cook just until slightly thickened, about 2 minutes. Combine macaroni and milk mixture with remaining ingredients except cracker crumbs. Pour into a buttered 3-quart casserole dish. Cover with cracker crumbs. Bake, covered, at 350 degrees for one hour, until golden. Serves 6 to 8.

Tuck packets of gravy and seasoning mix into a
napkin holder to keep the pantry tidy.

Farmhouse Egg Noodles

Angela Miller
Jefferson City, MO

These scrumptious homemade noodles have been a tradition in our family for many years. Unrolling the noodles has always been the children's job...they love helping out!

1 c. all-purpose flour
1 egg, beaten
3 T. milk

1/8 t. salt
3 to 4 14-1/2 oz. cans chicken
  broth

Place flour in a large bowl; make a well in the center and add egg, milk and salt. Slowly stir to mix in flour until a soft ball forms; knead in any remaining flour. Roll out dough on a floured surface to about 1/4-inch thick. Roll up dough jelly-roll style; slice across to cut noodles about 1/2-inch wide. Unroll noodles and pile them on a floured surface while waiting for broth to warm. In a large saucepan, bring broth to a boil. Drop noodles into broth. Cook until tender, about 8 to 10 minutes. Makes 4 to 6 servings.

Homemade chicken broth is simple to make. Whenever you simmer chicken for a recipe, save the liquid and freeze it. When it's time to make broth, thaw and combine with the desired amount of chopped onion, chopped carrots and sliced celery. Simmer, uncovered, for one hour and strain.

Tomato-Basil Pasta Bake

Lori Van Antwerp
Delaware, OH

*Your family will love the fresh taste of the homemade pasta sauce...
it's simple to make using canned tomatoes.*

2/3 c. onion, chopped
2 cloves garlic, minced
2 T. butter
28-oz. can diced tomatoes with
   Italian herbs
2 T. fresh basil, snipped
1/2 t. sugar

1/4 t. pepper
Optional: 1 T. capers, drained
8-oz. pkg. thin spaghetti,
   uncooked and divided
1/2 c. shredded mozzarella
   cheese

In a large skillet, sauté onion and garlic in butter until onion is tender.
Stir in tomatoes with juice and seasonings. Bring to a boil; reduce
heat. Simmer, uncovered, for about 20 minutes. Stir in capers, if
using; remove from heat. Meanwhile, measure out half the spaghetti,
reserving the rest for another recipe. Cook according to package
directions. Drain spaghetti and add to skillet; toss to coat with sauce.
Spoon into a lightly greased 9"x9" baking pan. Sprinkle with cheese.
Bake at 400 degrees for 5 to 8 minutes, or until bubbly and cheese
is melted. Serves 4.

Treat yourself to a bar or two of handmade herbal soap and
savor the scent everyday, not just in the bath! Keep a fragrant
bar of lemon verbena soap at the kitchen sink for quick
wash-ups or tuck an unwrapped bar of lavender soap
into a drawer of tea towels. Ahhh!

Spanish Hominy

Megan Brooks
Antioch, TN

Use either white or yellow hominy for this old-fashioned side.

2 29-oz. cans hominy, drained
14-1/2 oz. can diced tomatoes
10-oz. can diced tomatoes with
  chiles

8-oz. can tomato sauce
3/4 lb. bacon, diced
1 onion, chopped
1 green pepper, chopped

Combine hominy, both cans of tomatoes in juice and tomato sauce in a slow cooker; set aside. In a skillet over medium heat, cook bacon until crisp. Remove bacon to a paper towel-covered plate. Drain skillet, reserving one tablespoon drippings. Add onion and pepper; sauté until tender. Stir onion mixture and bacon into mixture in slow cooker. Cover and cook on low setting for 6 to 8 hours. Makes 8 to 10 servings.

Try your hand at vegetable gardening! Even the smallest yard is sure to have a sunny corner where you can grow sun-ripened tomatoes and an herb plant or two. Or, fill a wooden half-barrel with potting soil and plant a mini garden. Seeds, plants and free advice are available at the nearest garden store.

Tyler's Strawberry Tapioca

Maureen Froemming
Darwin, MN

I make this salad quite often when we get together for family birthday parties. It is my nephew Tyler's favorite salad. This is a great make-ahead recipe.

5 c. water
3/4 t. salt
1/2 c. plus 1 T. pearl tapioca, uncooked
1 c. sugar
3-oz. pkg. strawberry gelatin mix

8-oz. container frozen whipped topping, thawed
2 c. strawberries, hulled and sliced

In a large saucepan, combine water and salt. Bring to a boil over medium heat. Add tapioca; cook for 20 minutes. Remove from heat; stir in sugar and gelatin mix. Pour into a large serving bowl; cover and refrigerate overnight. At serving time, stir gelatin to break up; fold in whipped topping and berries. Makes 12 servings.

At country potlucks and carry-ins, fruity gelatin salads are yummy when topped with a dollop of creamy lemon mayonnaise. Stir 3 tablespoons each of lemon juice, light cream and powdered sugar into 1/2 cup mayonnaise. Garnish with a sprinkle of lemon zest, if you like.

Raspberry Pretzel Salad

Gean Wilson
Greenwater, WA

A neighbor shared this recipe with me during a neighborhood barbecue. Now I take this along to any barbecues I attend. The next day, people always call me to ask for the recipe.

1-1/2 c. pretzels, crushed
1/2 c. butter, melted
1 c. sugar, divided
8-oz. pkg. cream cheese, softened
8-oz. container frozen whipped topping, thawed

6-oz. pkg. raspberry gelatin mix
2 c. boiling water
2 10-oz. pkgs. frozen raspberries

Combine pretzels, melted butter and 1/2 cup sugar in a bowl; mix well. Press into the bottom of an ungreased 13"x9" baking pan to form a crust. Bake at 350 degrees for 5 to 7 minutes; let cool. Combine cream cheese, whipped topping and remaining sugar in a separate bowl; spread over baked crust. Cover and chill. Combine gelatin mix and boiling water in another bowl; stir well. Cover and chill until partially set. Stir frozen berries into gelatin; spread over cream cheese layer. Cover and refrigerate until serving time. Makes 12 to 15 servings.

Thrifty farm wives always used cotton kitchen towels...
they're still a great alternative to toss-away paper towels.
Dress up plain-Jane towels by stitching on narrow bands
of vintage quilting fabric and a row or two of rick rack.

Tried & True Apple Casserole

Gerry Donnella
Boston, VA

Whenever I would fry apples they turned out like applesauce, until a friend said, "I have a recipe you will love." She was right...I've been using it ever since and it NEVER fails! This is a great potluck dish.

8 to 10 tart apples, cored, peeled
   and halved
1/2 c. sugar
1/2 t. cinnamon

1/4 t. nutmeg
1 T. all-purpose flour
2 T. butter

Place apples in a buttered 2-quart casserole dish; set aside. Mix dry ingredients together; sprinkle over apples. Dot with butter. Cover and bake at 350 degrees for 45 minutes to one hour. Serves 6 to 8.

A vintage wooden soda crate makes a handy
spice rack...hang it on the wall or simply stand it up
on the kitchen counter.

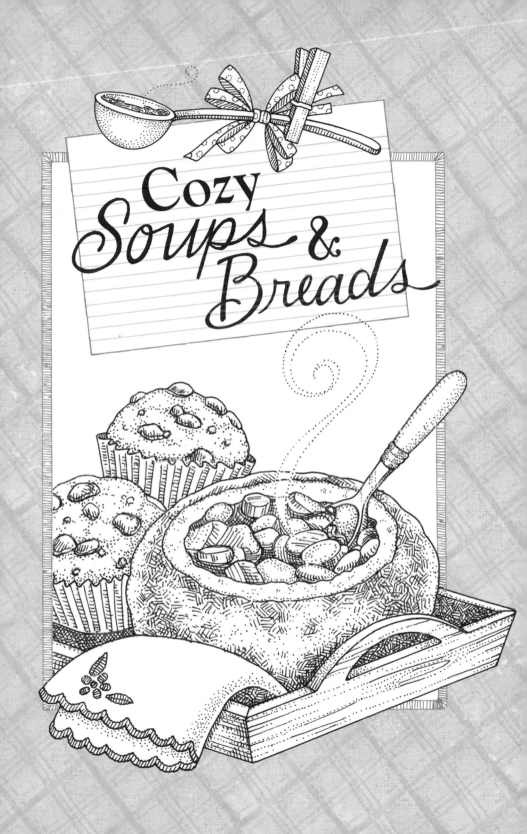

Cozy
Soups & Breads

Mushroom-Barley Soup

Holly Vidourek
Cincinnati, OH

Rich and hearty...always a family favorite.

1/2 lb. stew beef, cubed
1 onion, chopped
8-oz. pkg. sliced mushrooms

1 T. olive oil
4 14-1/2 oz. cans beef broth
3/4 c. instant barley, uncooked

Combine beef, onion, mushrooms and oil in a large saucepan. Cook over medium-high heat for about 10 minutes, until beef is browned. Stir in broth; bring to a boil. Add barley. Reduce heat and simmer, covered, for 30 to 45 minutes, until beef and barley are tender. Serves 4 to 6.

Yellowware soup bowls make any soup supper extra special. Pick up a set of vintage-style new bowls or collect old ones at antique shops...mix & match for fresh farmhouse style.

Cozy *Soups* & *Breads*

Potato Patch Soup

Corrie Leydig
Hyndman, PA

*This recipe is my mother's...every couple of weeks, she was sure
to have this soup waiting for us on the stove.*

7 potatoes, peeled and diced
1 carrot, peeled and finely
   chopped
2 T. dried, minced onion
3 c. water
4 cubes chicken bouillon

1 T. dried parsley
1 t. celery seed
4 slices pasteurized process
   cheese spread
1-1/2 c. milk

Combine potatoes, carrot, onion, water, bouillon cubes, parsley and
celery seed in a large saucepan. Simmer over medium heat until
potatoes are tender, 25 to 30 minutes. Remove from heat. Add cheese
slices; let stand until melted. Stir in milk and serve. Serves 5 to 7.

No matter where I serve my guests,
They seem to like my kitchen best.
–Old Saying

Cheese-Stuffed Biscuits

Angie Venable
Ostrander, OH

My kind of recipe...down-home goodness, ready to serve in a jiffy!

10-oz. tube refrigerated flaky
   biscuits
8-oz. pkg. Cheddar cheese,
   sliced into 10 cubes

1 T. milk
1 t. poppy seed

Separate dough into 10 biscuits. Open a small pocket in the side of
each biscuit; tuck a cheese cube into each pocket. Press dough
together to seal well. Place biscuits on an ungreased baking sheet. Cut
a deep "X" in the top of each biscuit. Brush with milk and sprinkle
with poppy seed. Bake at 400 degrees for 10 to 12 minutes, until
golden. Serve warm. Makes 10.

Slip a prewarmed ceramic tile into the bread basket
before adding a napkin liner. Biscuits and rolls will stay
toasty and warm through dinner.

Cozy Soups & Breads

Tomato & Basil Bisque

Zoe Bennett
Columbia, SC

Garnish servings with a swirl of cream and a sprig of basil leaves.

2 onions, chopped
2 carrots, peeled and shredded
1 T. butter
8 tomatoes, peeled and chopped
1/2 t. sugar

1/2 t. salt
1/4 t. pepper
1/2 c. fresh basil, chopped
2 c. chicken broth

In a large saucepan over medium heat, sauté onions and carrots in butter until tender. Stir in tomatoes, sugar, salt and pepper; bring to a boil. Reduce heat; cover and simmer for 10 minutes. Cool soup slightly; transfer to a blender. Add basil; cover and process until smooth. Pour soup back into saucepan. Stir in broth; heat through. Serves 4.

Dried celery leaves add homestyle flavor to soups and stews. Save the leaves from celery stalks, spread them on a baking sheet and dry slowly in a 180-degree oven for 3 hours. When they're crisp and dry, store them in a canning jar. The leaves can be crumbled right into a simmering soup pot.

Teri's Butternut Squash Soup

Teri Johnson
North Ogden, UT

We tried a delicious squash soup at a local restaurant. This recipe is my own version and it's so good! We find it's also good served chilled, with sliced green onions on top.

1 T. olive oil
1 T. butter
2 2-lb. butternut squash, peeled
   and cubed
1 onion, chopped

1 clove garlic, minced
1/2 t. allspice
2 14-1/2 oz. cans chicken broth
Garnish: sour cream, saltine
   crackers

Combine oil and butter in a large saucepan over medium heat. Add squash, onion and garlic. Cook for about 5 minutes, stirring occasionally, until crisp-tender. Add allspice; cook just a minute more. Add broth. Bring to a boil; cover. Reduce heat to low; simmer for 15 minutes, or until squash is tender. Mash with a potato masher or use an immersion stick blender to blend until smooth. Return to saucepan; heat until hot. If a thinner soup is preferred, add a little more broth or water. Ladle soup into 8 soup bowls. Add one tablespoon sour cream to each bowl and swirl slightly. Serve with crackers. Serves 8.

A pretty cut-glass biscuit jar isn't just for holding cookies or crackers...fill it with crisp bread sticks or pretzel rods to serve with soup.

Cream of Zucchini Soup

Susan Maurer
Dahlgren, IL

One taste and you'll agree...there's really no such thing
as too many zucchini!

3 lbs. zucchini, sliced
   1/2-inch thick
2 onions, quartered
5 slices bacon
4 c. chicken broth
1 t. salt

1 t. pepper
Optional: 1/2 t. garlic powder
Garnish: onion and garlic
   croutons or butter and
   grated Parmesan cheese

Combine all ingredients except garnish in a soup pot over medium heat. Cook until zucchini is tender and bacon is done, about 45 minutes. Ladle soup into a blender and process until smooth. Return to soup pot; heat through. Serve topped with croutons or with a pat of butter and a sprinkling of Parmesan cheese. Makes 4 to 6 servings.

Save time when peeling and chopping veggies. Set a large
bowl on the counter to toss all the peelings into...
you'll only need to empty it once.

Monk's Bean Soup

Staci Meyers
Montezuma, GA

My cousin Monk came to visit once and brought us a pot of this yummy soup. I wouldn't let him leave until he shared the recipe!

1 to 2 smoked ham hocks
6 to 8 c. water
2 T. butter
1 onion, chopped
3 to 5 T. dill weed

seasoned salt and pepper to taste
16-oz. pkg. dried Great Northern beans

Combine ham hocks and water in a large soup pot. Simmer over medium heat for 15 to 30 minutes. Melt butter in a skillet; add onion and seasonings. Cook for about 5 minutes, just until onion is tender. Place beans in a slow cooker; add onion mixture, then pour meat and broth over top. Cover and cook on high setting for 4 to 6 hours, until beans are as tender as desired. Shortly before serving time, dice meat from ham hocks and stir back into slow cooker. Makes 8 servings.

Pile seasonal produce in a primitive wooden dough bowl for a bountiful country-style centerpiece...shiny red and yellow peppers in summer, acorn squash and gourds in autumn.

Tadpole Ham Soup

Sara Goodroe
Moultrie, GA

A family recipe we've used for generations...the small onion pieces
gave this wonderful southern dish its funny name.

2 c. cooked ham, cubed
1 c. pan drippings from
   a baked ham
4 to 5 green onions, cut into
   one-inch pieces

4 c. water
pepper to taste

Put ham cubes, pan drippings, onions and water into a soup pot.
Bring to a slow boil over medium heat; simmer for 10 minutes. While
soup is boiling, drop dumplings by tablespoonfuls into the pot. Slowly
cook until dumplings are done, about 20 minutes. Add a little more
water if soup seems too thick. Add pepper to taste. Serves 4.

Dumplings:

1 egg, beaten

1 c. self-rising flour

Combine egg and flour, working them together by hand until
dough forms.

Stitch several handmade napkins or tea towels
end-to-end to make a one-of-a-kind table runner.

No-Knead Oatmeal Bread

Hattie Douthit
Crawford, NE

I've been making this bread since I was a little girl.
It's slightly sweet and so yummy.

2 envs. active dry yeast
1/2 c. warm water
1 c. quick-cooking oats,
   uncooked
1/2 c. light molasses
1/3 c. shortening

1-1/2 c. boiling water
1 T. salt
6-1/4 c. all-purpose flour,
   divided
2 eggs, beaten

Soften yeast in very warm water, 110 to 115 degrees; let stand for about 5 minutes. In a large bowl, combine oats, molasses, shortening, boiling water and salt; stir until shortening is melted. Cool until lukewarm. Stir in 2 cups of flour; add eggs and beat well. Stir in yeast mixture. Add remaining flour, 2 cups a time, mixing well after each addition to make a rather stiff dough. Beat vigorously until smooth, about 10 minutes. Grease top of dough lightly. Cover tightly; place in refrigerator for 2 hours to overnight. Turn dough out onto a well-floured surface. Form into 2 loaves; place in greased 8"x4" loaf pans. Cover; let rise in a warm place until double. Bake at 375 degrees for about 40 minutes. If crust begins to brown too fast, cover with aluminum foil for last half of baking time. Makes 2 loaves.

Here's how to tell when rising dough has doubled in size.
Press two fingertips into the dough, about 1/2-inch deep,
and then release. If the dent remains, the dough has doubled.

Honey Koek Loaf

Tawnia Hultink
Ontario, Canada

A nice easy-to-make Dutch bread...kids love it!

2 c. all-purpose flour
1 c. sugar
1 t. cinnamon
1/2 t. ground ginger
1/2 t. nutmeg
1/2 t. ground cloves

1 t. baking soda
1/2 t. baking powder
1/2 t. salt
1/2 c. honey
1 c. boiling water

Combine dry ingredients in a large bowl; mix all together. Add honey and boiling water; stir together. Pour batter into a greased 9"x5" loaf pan. Bake at 350 degrees for one hour. Cool in pan for 10 minutes; turn loaf out of the pan and cool on a wire rack. Makes one loaf.

Snap up stoneware butter crocks when you find them at flea markets. They're just the right size for serving party spreads and dips as well as butter.

Country Comfort Chicken Soup

Rhonda Nehmer
Menomonee Falls, WI

Everyone needs a great recipe for chicken noodle soup! I love homemade soup but do not have enough time anymore to spend hours making it, so I created this simpler version.

5 to 6 boneless, skinless
   chicken thighs
2 c. baby carrots, chopped
1 c. celery, chopped
1/2 onion, chopped
2 T. garlic, minced

1 t. poultry seasoning
1 t. dried parsley
1 t. seasoned salt
3 cubes chicken bouillon
12-oz. pkg. fine egg noodles,
   uncooked

Place all ingredients except noodles into a large soup pot; cover with water. Bring to a boil; reduce heat to a simmer. Cook, uncovered, until chicken and vegetables are tender, about one hour. Remove chicken; let cool slightly. Stir in noodles. Simmer until noodles are done, about 5 minutes. While noodles are cooking, dice chicken and return to soup. Adjust seasoning as needed. Makes 8 servings.

Savory herbed crackers make any bowl of soup even yummier! Toss together 1-1/2 cups oyster crackers, 1-1/2 tablespoons melted butter, 1/4 teaspoon dried thyme and 1/4 teaspoon garlic powder. Spread on a baking sheet. Bake at 350 degrees for about 10 minutes, until crunchy and golden.

Cider Mill Stew

Laura Lett
Delaware, OH

This stew smells as wonderful as it tastes!

3 T. all-purpose flour
1 t. salt
1/2 t. pepper
1 lb. stew beef, cubed
2 T. oil
1 c. apple cider
1 c. water
1 c. beef broth

1 T. cider vinegar
1/2 t. dried thyme
2 carrots, peeled and cut into
   1-inch pieces
1 stalk celery, cut into 1-inch
   pieces
1 potato, peeled and cubed
1 onion, sliced

Combine flour, salt and pepper in a large plastic zipping bag. Add beef, a few pieces at a time; shake to coat. In a Dutch oven, brown beef in oil; drain. Stir in cider, water, broth vinegar and thyme; bring to a boil over medium heat. Reduce heat; cover and simmer for one hour and 45 minutes, or until meat is tender. Add vegetables; return to a boil. Reduce heat; cover and simmer for 30 minutes, or until vegetables are tender. Makes 4 servings.

Turn a mesh bag that held apples or onions into a sink scrubbie for cleaning veggies and washing dishes. Simply fold the bag several times into a loose bundle and wind with kitchen string. So thrifty...Grandma would be proud!

Squash & Sausage Stew

Debbie Gillam
Tipton, IN

My great-aunts Ardella and Clarissa were avid gardeners, so they had an abundance of fresh veggies. They devised this fresh and nutritious soup recipe that I've made often. It's even tastier as leftovers!

1 lb. smoked turkey sausage,
    cut in bite-size pieces
2 to 3 yellow squash, cut into
    1/2-inch cubes
2 to 3 zucchini, cut into
    1/2-inch cubes

2 14-1/2 oz. cans diced
    tomatoes
1 onion, chopped
2 to 3 cloves garlic, minced

Combine all ingredients in a large soup pot. Bring to a boil over medium-high heat. Reduce heat to low. Simmer until vegetables are tender, stirring occasionally, one to 2 hours. Serves 4 to 6.

Keep a few quart-size Mason jars tucked in the cupboard so you can send home some homemade soup with a dinner guest...what a thoughtful gesture!

Down-Home Pea Soup

Jude Trimnal
Brevard, NC

Our parents made this soup often. It is delicious year 'round,
but is especially warming on winter days.

8 c. water
2 c. dried split peas
1-1/2 c. celery, sliced
1-1/2 c. carrots, peeled and
    sliced

1 onion, sliced
2 bay leaves
salt and pepper to taste
Optional: 1 to 2 c. cooked ham,
    cubed

Combine all ingredients in a slow cooker. Cover and cook on low
setting for 4 to 6 hours. Discard bay leaves before serving. Makes 8 to
10 servings.

Don't pass up delicious-sounding recipes that make enough
to serve a farmhouse family when you only need to serve two.
Leftovers are great for next-day meals. Soups, stews and
casseroles make quick & easy lunches, or freeze leftovers
for a heat-and-serve meal later when time is short.

Old-Fashioned Icebox Rolls

Muriel Gundy
Morley, MI

A very old tried & true recipe from my mother and aunt.
This is also a good dough to use for making cinnamon rolls.

1 env. active dry yeast	1/2 c. cold water
1/4 c. warm water	1/2 t. salt
1/2 c. boiling water	1 egg, beaten
1/3 c. shortening	3-3/4 c. all-purpose flour
1/3 c. sugar	

In a small bowl, combine yeast and very warm water, 110 to
115 degrees; let stand for several minutes. In a separate large bowl,
pour boiling water over shortening and sugar. Add yeast mixture, cold
water, salt, egg and flour. Mix and knead until smooth. Cover and
place in refrigerator overnight. Form into golfball-size balls and place
in a greased 13"x9" baking pan. Cover; let rise until double. Bake at
400 degrees for 12 to 18 minutes, until golden. Makes 2 dozen.

It's easy to turn a vintage painted metal tray into a whimsical
wall clock with a clock kit from your local craft store. Drill
a center hole, then insert the clock movement and hands.
Press on self-adhesive numbers...time's up!

Cozy Soups & Breads

North Woods Bean Soup

Sharon Demers
Dolores, CO

Here is a great soup to come home to on a brisk, cool evening.

1/2 lb. turkey Kielbasa, halved
    lengthwise and sliced
    1/2-inch thick
1 c. baby carrots, chopped
1 c. onion, chopped
2 cloves garlic, minced

4 c. chicken broth
1/2 t. Italian seasoning
1/2 t. pepper
2 15.8-oz. cans Great Northern
    beans, drained and rinsed
6-oz. pkg. baby spinach

Spray a large stockpot with non-stick vegetable spray; heat over medium-high heat. Add Kielbasa, carrots, onion and garlic; sauté for 3 minutes, stirring occasionally. Reduce heat to medium; cook for 5 minutes. Add broth, seasonings and beans. Bring to a boil; reduce heat and simmer for 5 minutes. Place 2 cups of soup in a blender or food processor. Process until smooth; return processed soup to pan. Simmer for an additional 5 minutes; remove from heat. Add spinach, stirring until it wilts. Serves 5.

Nothing goes better with hearty bean and pea soup than warm cornbread! If you like your cornbread crisp, prepare it in a vintage sectioned cast-iron skillet...each wedge of cornbread will bake up with its own golden crust.

Farmhouse Onion Soup

Irene Whatling
West Des Moines, IA

With four kinds of onions and two kinds of cheese,
this savory soup is a meal in itself.

2 T. butter
1 yellow onion, thinly sliced
1 red onion, thinly sliced
1 leek, white part only, sliced
5 green onions, sliced
1 clove garlic, minced
2 14-1/2 oz. cans beef broth

10-1/2 oz. can beef consommé
1 t. Worcestershire sauce
1/2 t. ground nutmeg
1 c. shredded Swiss cheese,
   divided
6 slices French bread, toasted
6 T. grated Parmesan cheese

Melt butter in a large saucepan over medium-low heat. Sauté all onions and garlic, stirring occasionally, until tender and golden, about 15 minutes. Add broth, consommé, Worcestershire sauce and nutmeg; bring to a boil. Reduce heat; cover and simmer for 30 minutes. Sprinkle one tablespoon Swiss cheese into each of 6 oven-proof soup bowls. Ladle soup into bowls; top each with a slice of toasted bread. Sprinkle bread with remaining Swiss and Parmesan. Broil until cheese is melted; serve right away. Serves 6.

A pretty china saucer that has lost its teacup can still
be useful. Place it beside the stovetop to serve as
a rest for cooking spoons and soup ladles.

Kale & Potato Soup

Maureen Viggiani
North Chili, NY

A quick, healthy soup for a blustery day. Make it heartier by adding 1/2 pound ground turkey sausage that has been browned and drained.

1 T. oil
1 onion, chopped
1/2 bunch kale, chopped

1 to 2 redskin potatoes, cubed
4 c. chicken broth

Heat oil in a medium saucepan over medium heat. Add onion and cook until translucent. Add kale, potato, broth and sausage, if using. Cover and simmer 15 minutes, until potato is tender. Serves 4 to 6.

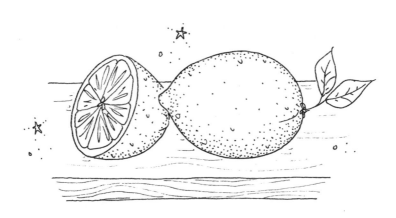

Use lemon juice to freshen an old wooden breadboard.
Brush juice generously over the surface and let stand
for 30 minutes. Then scrub with a moistened cloth
and a little baking soda, rinse and let dry.

Champion Banana Bread

Michelle Mahler
Osceola, WI

My grandma taught me most of what I know about baking. This simple recipe was hers...I wish I knew where she got it! I even won the Champion Ribbon at the county fair with this recipe when I was a young girl. My family belongs to a little old country church and it has been published in their cookbook several times as well.

2 eggs, beaten
1/2 c. butter, softened
1 c. sugar
3 bananas, mashed
1/2 c. evaporated milk

1 t. vanilla extract
1 t. baking powder
1 t. baking soda
1/2 t. salt
2 c. all-purpose flour

Blend eggs, butter and sugar; add bananas, milk and vanilla. Stir in dry ingredients; mix well. Pour batter into a 9"x5" loaf pan that has been sprayed with non-stick vegetable spray. Bake at 350 degrees for 40 to 50 minutes. Makes one loaf.

Make a new neighbor feel welcome by giving a loaf of homemade bread, wrapped in a checked napkin and tucked into a wicker basket.

Cozy Soups & Breads

Mom's Raisin Bread

Suzanne Pletsch
Chicago, IL

*Everyone loved Mom's raisin bread. When I got married,
Mom gave me the recipe...I finally got her to actually
measure ingredients! My children love it too.*

1 c. milk
1/4 c. margarine
2 t. salt
1/2 c. golden raisins
1 env. active dry rapid-rise yeast
2 T. sugar

1/2 c. warm water
2 eggs, beaten
5 c. all-purpose flour, divided
Garnish: beaten egg, milk or
softened margarine

In a small saucepan over low heat, heat milk just to boiling; stir in margarine and salt. Add raisins and let cool. In a large saucepan, combine yeast, sugar and very warm water, 110 to 115 degrees. When milk mixture cools, add it to yeast mixture; stir in eggs. Beat in flour, one cup at a time. When dough gets heavier, start to knead it, adding more flour if too sticky. Knead for about 10 minutes. Place dough in a large greased pan; cover. Set pan in an unheated oven with a pan of hot water placed below it. Let rise for one hour. Punch dough down; let rise for an additional 30 minutes. Knead dough again; form into 2 loaves and place in 2 greased 8-1/2"x4-1/2" loaf pans. Cover and let rise again for 30 minutes. Brush loaves with egg, milk or margarine. Bake at 375 degrees until golden, 45 to 60 minutes. Makes 2 loaves.

Grandma's little secret...kneading bread dough is a fun way
to get rid of stress! Be sure to knead the dough as long
as the recipe states, until the dough is silky smooth.
You'll be rewarded with moist, tender bread.

Chunky Minestrone

Sharon Ignash
Kinde, MI

This recipe has been a huge hit at soup luncheons, at family gatherings and at work. It's easy to make and low calorie for calorie watchers. We all just love it and hope you will too!

1 T. olive oil
1-1/2 c. onion, chopped
1 carrot, peeled and sliced
2 cloves garlic, minced
14-1/2 oz. can diced tomatoes
4 c. chicken broth
1 c. water
1 t. Italian seasoning

1/2 c. long-cooking rice or soup pasta, uncooked
15-oz. can kidney beans, drained and rinsed
1 zucchini, chopped
1/2 t. pepper
Garnish: grated Parmesan cheese

In a Dutch oven, heat oil over medium heat. Add onion, carrot and garlic; cook for 3 minutes, or until tender. Stir in tomatoes with juice, broth, water, seasoning and uncooked rice or pasta. Bring to a boil. Reduce heat and simmer, uncovered, for 20 minutes or until rice or pasta is tender. Stir in beans, zucchini and pepper; simmer for 5 minutes. Sprinkle with cheese before serving. Makes 5 servings.

Keep hard grating cheeses like Parmesan fresh for longer.
Wrap the cheese in a paper towel that has been
moistened with cider vinegar, tuck into a
plastic zipping bag and refrigerate.

Cozy Soups & Breads

Meatball Vegetable Soup

Sally Derkenne
Chandler, AZ

The made-from-scratch meatballs are really tasty,
but if time is short, substitute frozen meatballs.

4 c. beef broth
2-1/2 c. water
4 stalks celery, chopped
4 carrots, peeled and chopped
1 onion, chopped
1/4 c. quick-cooking barley,
    uncooked

8-oz. can tomato sauce
1 t. dried basil
2 cubes beef bouillon
3 potatoes, peeled and cubed
salt and pepper to taste

Combine broth and water in a large soup pot. Add celery, carrots, onion, barley, tomato sauce and basil; bring to a boil. Reduce heat; partially cover and simmer for 15 minutes. Add meatballs; cover and cook for 15 minutes. Add potatoes and cook until tender, about 20 minutes. Add salt and pepper to taste. Serves 6.

Meatballs:

1-1/2 lbs. ground beef
1/2 c. cooked rice
1 onion, finely chopped
1 egg, beaten

1/4 c. water
1 clove garlic, minced
salt and pepper to taste

Combine all ingredients in a large bowl; mix well. Shape into small meatballs.

Hang a flea-market-find window shutter on the wall to hold greeting cards, cookbooklets or catalogs. Add a row of cup hooks along the bottom to keep potholders at your fingertips.

Grandma's Irish Soda Bread

Jennifer Savino
Joliet, IL

My grandma was 100 percent Irish and she knew how to make the best Irish soda bread around. Serve it warm from the oven, topped with a pat of butter...there's nothing better!

3 c. all-purpose flour
2/3 c. sugar
1 t. baking powder
1 t. baking soda
1 t. salt

1-1/2 c. raisins
2 eggs, beaten
1-3/4 c. buttermilk
2 T. butter, melted and slightly
    cooled

Sift dry ingredients together in a large bowl; stir in raisins and set aside. In a separate bowl, combine eggs, buttermilk and melted butter, blending well. Add egg mixture to flour mixture; stir until well mixed. Pour batter into two greased 9"x5" loaf pans. Bake at 350 degrees for one hour. Turn loaves out of pans and let cool on a wire rack. Makes 2 loaves.

Making butter is fun for kids. Pour a pint of heavy cream into a chilled wide-mouth jar, cap the jar tightly and take turns shaking until you see butter begin to form. When it's done, uncap the jar and rinse the butter lightly with cool water. Enjoy on warm, fresh-baked bread...yum!

PatPat's Pot of Soup

PatPat Storey
Cleveland, TN

This soup is quick & easy for friends and fellowship any night of the week! Just leave the slow cooker set on low until you get home from work. Serve with a basket of cornbread or corn chips...it's great either way!

15-1/2 oz. can chili with beans
15 1/2 oz. can chili without
    beans
15-1/4 oz. can corn

10-3/4 oz. can tomato soup
10-oz. can tomatoes with chiles
Garnish: shredded Cheddar
    cheese, sour cream

Combine all ingredients except garnish in a slow cooker. Cover and cook on low for 6 to 8 hours, until steaming hot. Serve soup portions garnished with cheese and sour cream. Serves 4.

A vintage-style oilcloth tablecloth with brightly colored fruit and flowers adds cheer to any dinner table. Its wipe-clean ease makes it oh-so practical for any meal of the day.

Spicy Sausage & Kale Soup

Sarah Gruber
Monroe, MI

I love to make soup from scratch! When my youngest daughter was expecting her first baby, I created this soup for her. She said it was so good I should enter it in a contest! Serve it with warm crusty garlic bread for a really satisfying meal.

6 slices bacon, diced
1 onion, chopped
2 to 3 cloves garlic, minced
4 c. chicken broth
3 c. water or chicken broth
3 potatoes, peeled and diced
2 to 3 c. kale, chopped
14-1/2 oz. can diced tomatoes
   with chiles

15-oz. can chickpeas, drained
1/2 t. garlic powder
1/2 t. onion powder
1 lb. smoked pork sausage,
   halved lengthwise and sliced
   1/2-inch thick
1 c. whipping cream
salt and pepper to taste

In a large stockpot, cook bacon until crisp. Remove to paper towels and drain, reserving 2 tablespoons drippings. Add onion and garlic; sauté in reserved drippings until softened. Add broth, water or broth, potatoes, kale, tomatoes with chiles, chickpeas, garlic powder and onion powder. Bring to a boil; reduce heat and simmer until potatoes and kale are cooked through, about 15 to 20 minutes. Meanwhile, broil or fry sausage until browned; drain. Stir reserved bacon, sausage and cream into soup. Heat gently for an additional 5 minutes; add salt and pepper as needed. Makes 10 servings.

There's nothing like soup for turning leftovers into a hot, hearty meal. Keep a container in the freezer for extra chopped vegetables, roast beef, shredded chicken or even crispy bacon. When you have saved enough, just add a couple of cans of broth and a can of diced tomatoes. Simmer until everything blends together...scrumptious!

Cozy Soups & Breads

Farmstand Bacon-Corn Soup

Barbara Pache
Marshall, WI

This creamy, savory soup really hits the spot in chilly weather!
Everyone who tries it wants the recipe, so I thought
*I would share it with other **Gooseberry Patch** fans.*

1 butternut squash
12 slices bacon, diced
1 onion, chopped
1 stalk celery, chopped
1 T. all-purpose flour
14-1/2 oz. can chicken broth
2 14-3/4 oz. cans creamed corn

2 8-oz. cans corn, drained
1 pt. half-and-half
1 T. fresh parsley, minced
1-1/2 t. salt
1/2 t. pepper
Optional: sour cream

Place squash on an ungreased baking sheet. Bake at 375 degrees for one hour. Cut in half; cool. Remove seeds with a spoon; scoop out pulp and mash. Set aside. In a large saucepan over medium-high heat, cook bacon until crisp. Remove bacon to paper towels, reserving 2 tablespoons drippings in saucepan. Sauté onion and celery until tender. Stir in flour; blend well. Gradually stir in 6 cups squash and remaining ingredients except sour cream; return crumbled bacon to saucepan. Cook and stir over low heat until heated through. Garnish with dollops of sour cream, if desired. Serves 8.

Enjoy a favorite long-simmering recipe more often...let a slow cooker do the work for you! Brown and drain ground meat first, then toss all ingredients into the slow cooker. A soup that cooks for 2 hours on the stovetop can cook all day on the low setting without burning or overcooking.

Yummy Carrot-Raisin Muffins

Nancy Haines
Hicksville, NY

*This recipe for extra-moist muffins was a wonderful gift from
my secret pal! Substitute other flavors of cake mix too...
devil's food, orange and spice cake all make tasty muffins.*

18-oz. pkg. carrot cake mix   1/3 c. golden raisins
15-oz. can pumpkin

Mix dry cake mix and pumpkin together to make a very thick batter.
Add raisins and mix well. Fill paper-lined muffin cups 2/3 full. Bake
at 400 degrees for 20 minutes, until muffins test done. Makes
one dozen.

An old-fashioned ice cream scoop isn't handy just for
serving up frozen treats. Use it for scooping muffin
batter, mashed potatoes and even jumbo meatballs...
you'll have perfect portions every time!

Cozy Soups & Breads

Butterfly Yeast Rolls

Janis Parr
Ontario, Canada

*I have been baking these delicious rolls for years and they are the best!
The rolls rise to perfection and are golden and flaky...
sure to delight family & friends.*

1 env. active dry yeast
1/4 c. warm water
1 c. milk
1/4 c. sugar
1/4 c. shortening

1 t. salt
3-1/2 c. all-purpose flour,
   divided
1 egg, beaten

In a small bowl, mix yeast with very warm water, 110 to
115 degrees; let stand for 5 minutes. Heat milk in a small saucepan
over low heat just until boiling; let cool slightly. In a large bowl,
combine milk, sugar, shortening and salt. Add 1-1/2 cups flour and
beat well. Beat in yeast mixture and egg. Gradually knead in
remaining flour to form a soft dough. Place in a greased bowl, turning
once. Cover and let rise in a warm place for 2 hours. Punch dough
down; turn out on a floured surface. Shape into 36 walnut-size balls;
place 3 balls in each cup of a greased muffin tin. Cover and let rise for
45 minutes. Bake at 400 degrees for 12 to 15 minutes, or until
golden. Makes one dozen.

Give homebaked rolls and bread a mouthwatering golden
finish. Whisk together an egg yolk and a tablespoon of water
in a cup. Brush the mixture over the dough just before
sliding it into the oven...it's as simple as that.

Crawfish-Corn Chowder

Becky Garrett
Richardson, TX

As displaced Cajuns from Lousiana now living in Texas, my family loves this chowder...it's a delicious reminder of home.

12-oz. pkg. bacon, crisply
   cooked, crumbled and
   drippings reserved
2 c. potatoes, peeled and diced
1 c. onion, diced
2 T. butter
2 pts. half-and-half

2 16-oz. cans creamed corn
1 T. Creole seasoning
Optional: 1 t. hot pepper sauce
1 lb. frozen crawfish tails or
   uncooked medium shrimp,
   peeled

Place 4 tablespoons reserved drippings in a soup pot. Sauté potatoes and onion for about 15 minutes, until golden. Stir in butter, half-and-half, corn, seasoning and hot sauce, if using. Add crumbled bacon to chowder. Cook over medium heat until potatoes are tender, 20 to 30 minutes. Add crawfish or shrimp and simmer for another 15 to 20 minutes; do not overcook. Serves 6 to 8.

Enamelware dishpans are so useful in the kitchen...don't pass them by at barn sales! They're perfect for mixing up company-size batches of bread dough, cookies, tossed salad, turkey dressing and so much more...even for serving popcorn on family movie night!

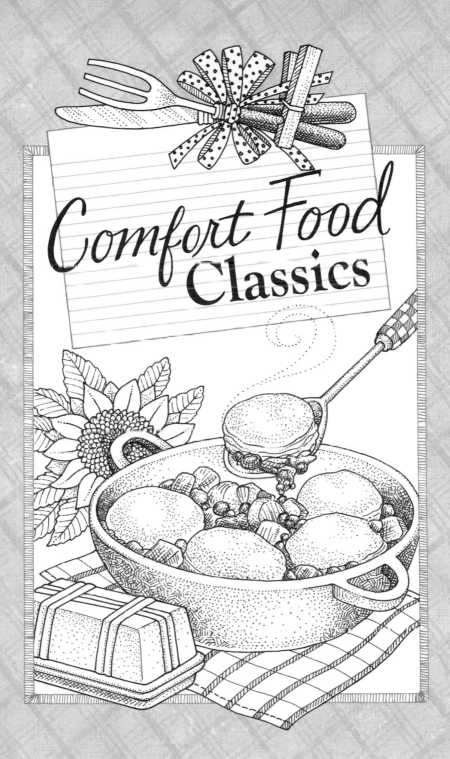

Comfort Food
Classics

Angie's Pot Roast with Buttermilk Gravy

Lisa Stanish
Houston, TX

My best friend gave me this recipe and it is the absolute best roast I have ever had. Since then, I've shared the recipe with other friends countless times. Spoon the gravy from the slow cooker over mashed potatoes...pure comfort food!

3-lb. beef chuck roast
3 T. oil
1 onion, chopped
3 T. all-purpose flour
1 c. buttermilk

1 c. water
4 T. beef bouillon granules
1/2 t. dried thyme
1/2 t. pepper

In a large skillet over medium-high heat, brown roast in oil on all sides. Remove roast to a slow cooker, reserving drippings; top roast with onion and set aside. Add flour to drippings in skillet; cook and stir until brown. Add buttermilk, water, bouillon, thyme and pepper; cook and stir until thickened. Pour gravy over roast and onion in slow cooker. Cover and cook on low setting for 5 to 7 hours. Serves 6.

Whip up a pretty tablecloth in no time by using a pretty patterned sheet. Just cut it to fit the table, hem it and trim the edges with ribbon or rick rack.

Shepherd's Pie

Donna Jenkins
Dayton, OH

My husband, a self-proclaimed meat & potatoes man, always requests this hearty one-dish favorite. The fact that it's simple to make and easy on the wallet makes it that much better.

1 onion, diced
1 to 2 t. oil
1 lb. ground beef
10-3/4 oz. can cream of
    mushroom soup
11-oz. can corn, drained

4 potatoes, peeled and cubed
1/4 c. milk
2 to 3 t. butter, sliced
salt and pepper to taste
3/4 c. shredded Cheddar or
    American cheese

In a skillet over medium heat, sauté onion in oil. Add ground beef and cook until no longer pink; drain. In a large bowl, mix beef, soup and corn; pour into a greased 8"x8" baking pan and set aside. Place potatoes in a saucepan; cover with water. Boil over medium-high heat until tender, about 10 minutes. Drain; add milk, butter, salt and pepper to pan. Whip potatoes with a potato masher or electric mixer and spread over beef mixture. Bake, covered, at 350 degrees for 30 minutes. Sprinkle with cheese and bake, uncovered, an additional 5 minutes. Serves 4.

Pickle jars, penny candy jars and glass pantry jars are so collectible! Use them in your kitchen to hold everything from pasta to cookies. They're great in the craft room, too...buttons, bobbins and spools will all be at home in these old-time containers.

Company Baked Ziti

Colleen Leid
Narvon, PA

Oh-so simple to put together, yet everyone loves it!

1 lb. ground beef
1 lb. sweet Italian ground
   pork sausage
1 onion, chopped
2 26-1/2 oz. cans spaghetti
   sauce
16-oz. pkg. ziti pasta, cooked

6-oz. pkg. sliced provolone
   cheese
1 c. sour cream
1-1/2 c. shredded mozzarella
   cheese
Garnish: grated Parmesan
   cheese

Brown beef, sausage and onion together in a skillet; drain. Stir in sauce; reduce heat to low and simmer for 15 minutes. Layer in a greased 13"x9" baking pan as follows: half of pasta, provolone cheese, sour cream, half of sauce mixture, remaining pasta, mozzarella cheese and remaining sauce. Top with Parmesan cheese. Cover and bake at 350 degrees for 30 minutes, or until hot, bubbly and cheeses are melted. Serves 6 to 8.

The art of being happy lies in the power of
extracting happiness from common things.
–Henry Ward Beecher

Comfort Food Classics

Ted's Favorite Meatballs

Susie Backus
Delaware, OH

These are delicious...great served over buttered noodles.
Very different from your average meatball!

2 lbs. ground beef
1-1/2 c. bread crumbs
1-1/2 oz. pkg. onion soup mix
8-oz. container sour cream
1 egg, beaten
1/3 c. all-purpose flour

1 t. paprika
1/4 c. butter
10-3/4 oz. can cream of chicken
   soup
3/4 c. milk

Mix ground beef, crumbs, soup mix, sour cream and egg in a large bowl; form into walnut-size meatballs. Combine flour and paprika; roll meatballs in mixture. Melt butter in a large skillet over medium-high heat. Brown meatballs; drain. Blend soup and milk together and pour over browned meatballs. Cover and simmer for about 20 minutes. Makes 6 to 8 servings.

Making lots of mini meatballs? Grab a melon baller and start scooping...you'll be done in record time!

Saucy Pork Chop Scallop

Hope Yates
Wesley, AR

*This recipe was handed down from my grandmother to my mother
and then to me. It is very simple, yet is oh-so creamy and good.*

4 pork chops
1 T. oil
salt and pepper to taste
10-3/4 oz. can cream of
   mushroom soup

1/2 c. sour cream
1/4 c. water
2 T. dried, minced onion
4 c. potatoes, peeled and
   thinly sliced

In a skillet over medium heat, brown pork chops in oil. Drain; sprinkle
with salt and pepper. Blend together soup, sour cream, water, onion,
potatoes and additional salt and pepper. Spread into a lightly greased
13"x9" baking pan. Top with browned pork chops. Cover; bake at
375 degrees for one hour and 15 minutes. Serves 4.

When pork chops are on the menu, sprinkle a little salt in
your cast-iron skillet before adding the oil and the meat.
You'll have less spattering and more flavorful pork chops.

Comfort Food Classics

Sweet-and-Sauerkraut Brats

Jo Ann
Gooseberry Patch

*I like to pop this into the slow cooker on Saturday mornings. Later,
when I get home from a day of barn sale-ing with friends,
I know a hearty meal will be ready to serve my family!*

1 1/2 to 2 lbs. bratwurst, cut
   into bite-size pieces
27-oz. can sauerkraut
4 tart apples, cored, peeled
   and chopped

1/4 c. onion, chopped
1/4 c. brown sugar, packed
1 t. caraway seed
4 to 6 hard rolls, split
Garnish: spicy mustard

Place bratwurst into a slow cooker. Toss together sauerkraut with
juice, apples, onion, brown sugar and caraway seed; spoon over
bratwurst. Cover and cook on low setting for 4 to 5 hours, stirring
occasionally. Fill rolls, using a slotted spoon. Serve with mustard on
the side. Makes 4 to 6 servings.

Whip up some whimsical fridge magnets. Glue round cut-outs
from family photos into retro pop bottle caps. Add button
magnets to the back with a dab of hot glue.

Easy Turkey & Dumplings

Tori Willis
Champaign, IL

A scrumptious way to serve leftover roast turkey! Spoon into soup plates and add a scattering of chopped fresh green parsley.

1 lb. roast turkey breast, cubed
1/4 c. carrot, peeled and
   chopped
1/4 c. onion, chopped

1/4 c. celery, chopped
3 c. turkey or chicken broth
salt and pepper to taste
12-oz. tube refrigerated biscuits

Place turkey, vegetables and broth in a medium saucepan; bring to a boil over medium heat. Reduce heat to low; simmer for 30 minutes, adding salt and pepper to taste. Pat out biscuits together on a lightly floured surface; cut into 2-inch by one-inch pieces. Drop biscuit pieces into the simmering broth. Cook over low heat for 10 to 15 minutes, until dumplings are done. Serve ladled into bowls. Makes 4 to 6 servings.

Add some whimsy to plain-Jane window shades...
simply use fabric glue to attach vintage sewing trim
like rick rack or pompom fringe along the edge.